Macramé Bags

Interweave

An imprint of Penguin Random House LLC
penguinrandomhouse.com

MUSUNDE TSUKURU MACRAMÉ BAG TO KOMONO
Copyright © 2018 Chizu Takuma

Original Japanese edition published by SEIBUNDO
SHINKOSHA PUBLISHING CO., LTD
English language licensed by World Book Media LLC, USA
via Tuttle-Mori Agency, Inc., Tokyo, Japan.

Production: Akiko Takuma, Sakie Takuma,
Taiga Takuma, Mai Takuma, Mariko Miyanishi
Photography: Daisuke Yoshida
Styling: Miki Uera
Design: Sayaka Higashimura (WILD PITCH)
Model: Sonia
Hair & Makeup: Ayami Yamada
Instructions: Shirokuma Kobo & Rika Tanaka
Illustrations: Tama Studio
Editor: Rie Suzuki (TAND)
English Editor: Lindsay Fair
Tech Editor: Amie Phillips-Krug
Translation: Kyoko Matthews
English Edition Design: Stacy Wakefield-Forte

Printed in China

10 9 8 7 6 5 4 3 2 1

ISBN: 978-0-59342-231-1

ABOUT THE AUTHOR

As a child, Chizu Takuma learned the art of macramé from her mother. Chizu rediscovered her love for macramé in her mid-20s and has been working as a fiber artist ever since. She is a lecturer at the Japan Macramé Promotion Association and regularly holds macramé workshops in Japan. Chizu enjoys making macramé projects alongside her mother, sister, daughter, and son. She lives in Nara, Japan.

Macramé Bags

21 stylish bags,
purses & accessories to make

Chizu Takuma

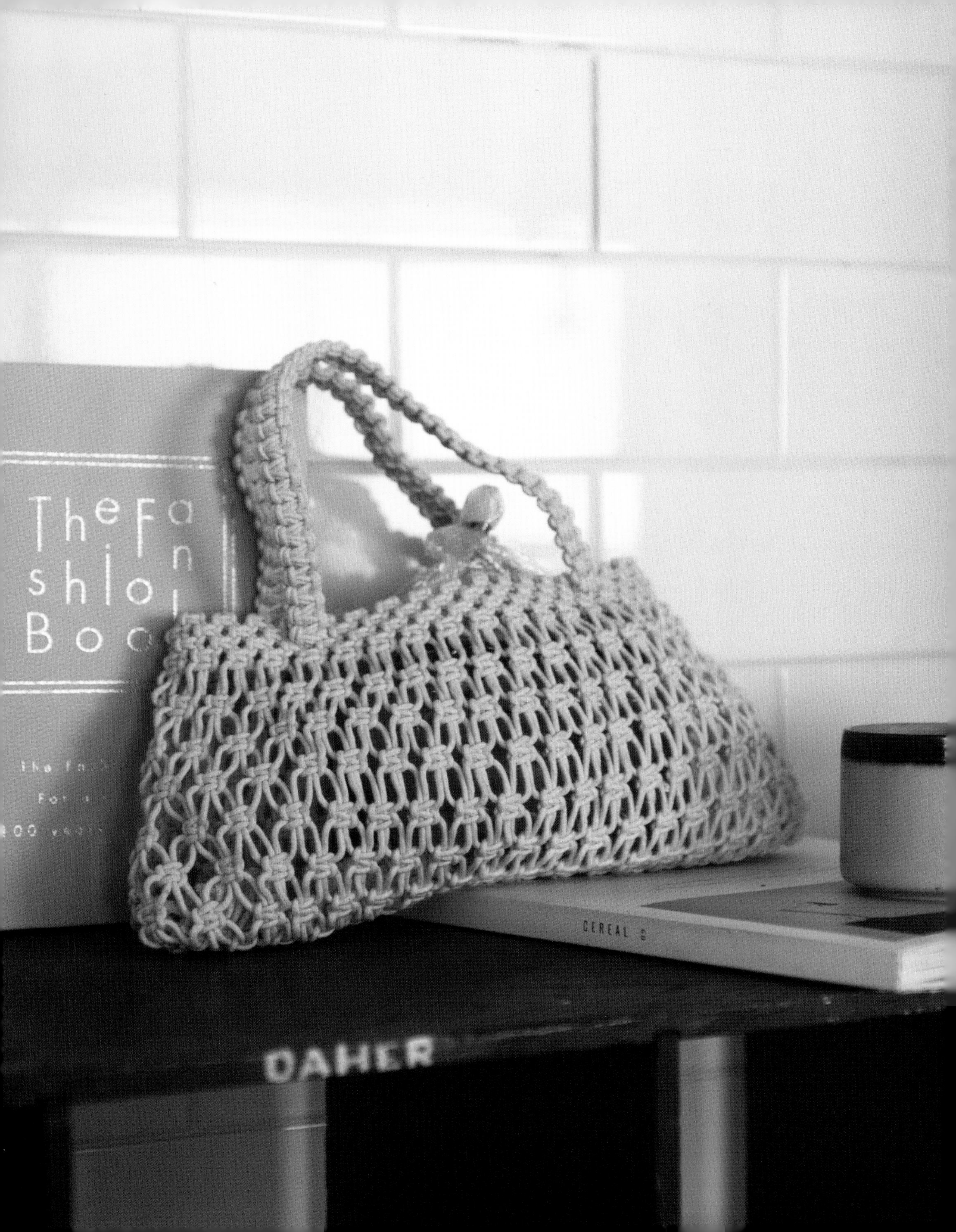
CEREAL
DAHER

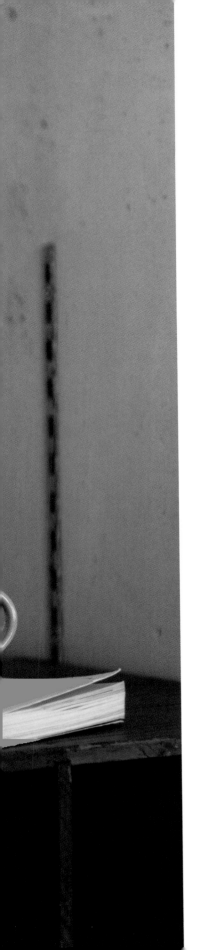

Macramé is a traditional handcraft that has been practiced around the world for centuries. It involves tying a series of knots to create decorative textiles. By combining just a handful of basic knots, you can create an almost endless variety of patterns.

You can use just about any type of string for macramé—hemp or cotton will create a natural look, while nylon will produce a lightweight, shiny finish. I recommend getting started with whatever cord you have lying around. Besides a pair of scissors and some pins, you don't need any fancy tools or equipment.

Once you master the basic techniques, just repeat the knots—that's how simple it is to make macramé!

I hope you enjoy making the bags and accessories included in this book. These useful items were designed to bring the beauty of macramé into everyday life!

contents

the projects

01

Black Net Purse with Leather Handles

instructions ▷ **page 76**

With its square knots and open structure, this bag is a quick project and is great for macramé beginners. The functional lining hides the bag's contents and keeps small items safely stored inside.

02

White Net Purse with Leather Handles

instructions ▷ **page 76**

Try using white cording and natural leather handles to create a softer impression of the same design used on page 10. The lighter color scheme makes this purse ideal for summer.

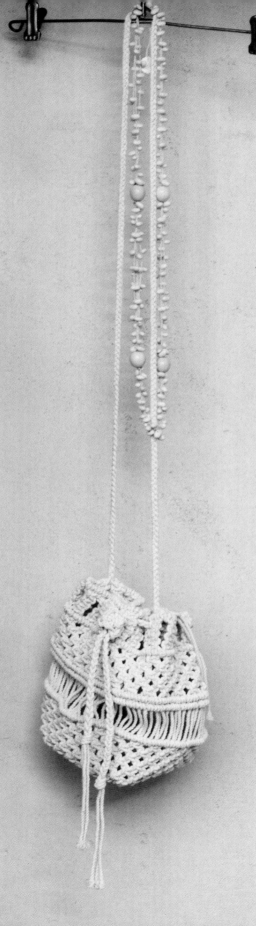

03

Cross-Body Drawstring Bag

instructions ▷ **page 80**

Combine square knots, treasure mesh panel, and clove hitch knots to create a unique bag made entirely from macramé cord. With a long cross-body strap and lightweight feel, this purse is perfect to wear while running errands or traveling.

04

Diagonal Clove Hitch Clutch

instructions ▷ **page 83**

Combine treasure mesh panel with diagonal clove hitch knots to create this interesting textural pattern, which is captivating even when worked in a single color of cord. Try a bold shade, such as the vibrant yellow shown here.

05

Popcorn
Purse

instructions ▷ **page 86**

Dark wood handles and a
rich color scheme give this
bag a vintage look. Work
nine consecutive berry
knots to create the fun,
three-dimensional bobble
pattern reminiscent of
popcorn.

a good beginning
makes a good

The treasure mesh panel may look complex, but it's actually quite simple to make as it's composed of alternating square or spiral knots. Bags 6-9 all feature treasure mesh patterns, but utilize varying cords and spacing. By changing these elements, you can create a variety of bag styles.

06

Treasure Mesh Bag

instructions ▷ **page 88**

Incorporate open space between the knots to create a stretchable bag. This design features gussets, which allow you to store more inside than you might expect.

07

Net Bag with Wooden Handles

instructions ▷ **page 92**

This vintage-inspired bag is constructed with jute cord and ring-shaped wooden handles, which will patina over time. For a different impression, try using a brighter color cord, such as green or yellow.

sac
papier merci

peut contenir

tention, votre jea

tes, **votre cœur,**

rs, vos santiags,

votre confiance,

é, votre pyjama,

s, **vos désirs,**

s disques,

re soutien...

ris

2 77 00 33

08

Mod Net Purse

instructions ▷ **page 94**

This design features rows of double square knots that create an airy treasure mesh pattern. This small purse is perfect for storing a wallet or paperback novel and is ideal for macramé beginners.

Nylon Market Tote

instructions ▷ **page 96**

This treasure mesh panel, which is composed of square knots, is beautiful and easy to make. By changing the space between the knots or using another type of rope, you can create a completely different style. This durable tote is made with lightweight nylon cord and is perfect for hauling farmer's market finds.

11

10 · 11

Solid & Striped Knit Pouches

instructions ▷ **pages 98 and 100**

Hand-dyed yarn, which has subtle shading and a smooth texture, lends these little pouches an artistic feel. The size is perfect for storing cosmetics or credit cards.

12 · 13

Diamond Tassel Clutches

instructions ▷ **page 102 and 105**

These beautiful and useful zippered pouches feature a decorative diamond motif made from clove hitch knots set among a simple square knot background. Add a tassel to the zipper pull for an even more custom look.

Projects 14-17 are versatile designs that can be used as belts or as bag straps. Incorporate these accessories into your wardrobe for chic summery style.

14 · 15

Zigzag Pattern Bag Strap & Six Strand Braid Bag Strap

instructions ▷ **pages 108 and 111**

Attach metal rings to the end of the strap or simply tie to the bag if it has grommets or loops. If you leave the cord ends long, they act as fringe and will swing as you walk!

14

15

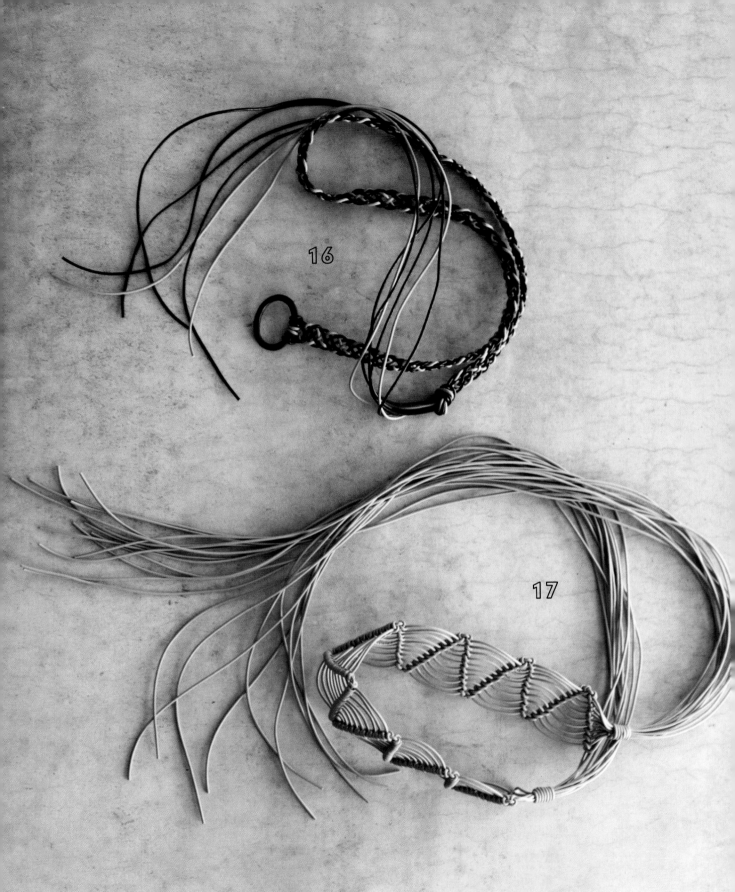

16

17

16 · 17

Six Strand Braid Belt
& Zigzag Pattern Belt

instructions ▷ **pages 108 and 111**

The wider belt shown on page 38 features a bold zigzag pattern that combines knots and openwork for a bohemian look. For a more sophisticated belt, try the narrower six strand braid version shown below.

16

18

Fringe Shoulder Bag

instructions ▷ **page 113**

This shoulder bag features beautiful diamond motifs and long, elegant fringe. Adjust the length of the strap to transform this design into a cross-body bag.

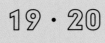

19 · 20

Nylon & Jute
Flat Bags

instructions ▷ **page 117**

Just three simple knots are used to
construct these elegant clutch bags—
the secret is to form the knots tightly
so the bag will keep its shape. Opt for
a single color of cord for a chic look.

20

19

 friend of mine owns a vintage shop in Tokyo called Oz Vintage. She inherited a beautiful macramé bag from the 1920s, pictured on the opposite page. The color of the bag may have faded over the years, but it possesses a special charm of its own. Here, we have replicated the pattern so macramé lovers around the world can create their own future heirloom.

21
Vintage-Inspired Handbag

instructions ▷ **page 120**

Use fine cotton cord to create the detailed pattern for this bag. Its classic shape makes the bag an elegant addition to a more formal outfit, but you can change the length of the strap to transform it into a more casual shoulder bag.

Modern Remake

Vintage

getting started ▷

About Cord

Just about any type of cord can be used for macramé. Natural fibers such as cotton, linen, hemp, and jute offer an earthy texture. Nylon cord is lightweight and has a unique sheen, while leather cord provides a sophisticated finish. Experiment to find your favorite materials and colors to create one-of-a-kind bags.

TIP

Wind Cord Into Bundles

Cord is often sold in skeins, which tend to tangle easily. Wind the cord around your fingers in a figure eight shape as shown in the photos below to create a neat, easy-to-use bundle.

Tools

One of the best things about macramé is that it doesn't require a lot of specialized tools or fancy equipment. In fact, you may have most of the things you'll need on hand already. In addition to cord, you may also want to purchase a good quality macramé board and some t-pins. You can make do with whatever type of board and pins you already have, but having the proper tools will increase your motivation and bring you one step closer to finishing your first bag.

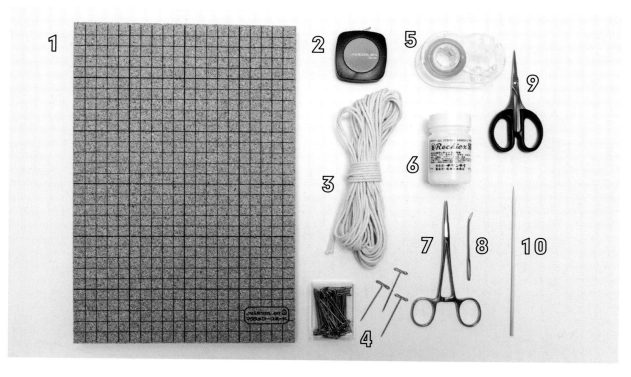

1 **Macramé board** Use a corkboard to secure cords and make the knotting process easier. Boards designed specifically for macramé are printed with grids, allowing you to easily measure the space between knots. If you don't have a macramé board, you can use a corkboard, cardboard, or even an ironing board!

2 **Tape measure** Use to measure the length of cords and the size of the bag.

3 **Cord** A variety of cords can be used for macramé. See page 48 for more information on the types of cord used in this book.

4 **T-pins** Use to attach cords to the board.

5 **Tape** If your cords unravel easily, wrap the ends with tape before cutting.

6 **Glue** Use a strong craft glue to securely finish cord ends.

7 **Forceps** Use to pull cords through tight spaces between knots.

8 **Tapestry needle** Use to finish cord ends by weaving under knots on the wrong side of the work.

9 **Scissors** Use to cut pieces of cord. Opt for a sharp pair designated exclusively for crafting.

10 **Bamboo skewer** Use to apply glue when finishing cord ends.

Starting Methods

Many of the projects in this book use one of the four basic macramé starting methods. Refer back to this guide when getting started with the individual projects in the book.

Starting Method A

Use this method to attach a working cord to an anchor cord, which is a foundation cord that spans the top of the work.

1 Fold the working cord in half and position it under the anchor cord with the loop pointing up.

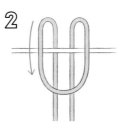

2 Bring the folded loop toward you.

3 Pull the cord ends through the loop and tighten.

Starting Method B

This method is very similar to method A above, but the loop of the finished knot is visible.

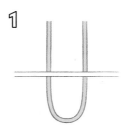

1 Fold the working cord in half and position it under the anchor cord with the loop pointing down.

2 Insert the working cord ends through the loop.

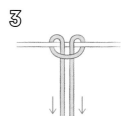

3 Pull the cord ends to tighten.

Starting Method C

This method builds upon method A, adding an extra wrap on one side of the knot for a wider starting point.

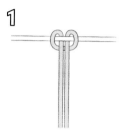

1 Follow steps 1-3 of method A on page 50.

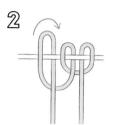

2 Wrap the left cord end around the anchor cord one more time.

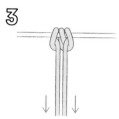

3 Pull the two cord ends to tighten.

Starting Method D

This method builds upon method A, adding an extra wrap on both sides of the knot to create an even wider starting point.

1 Follow steps 1-3 of method A on page 50.

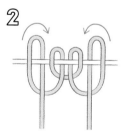

2 Wrap the left and right cord ends around the anchor cord one more time.

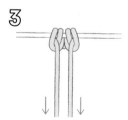

3 Pull the two cord ends to tighten. There should be a total of four wraps around the anchor cord.

Knot Guide

The following guide introduces the basic knotting techniques used in this book. Each technique includes a photo of the finished knot, as well as a symbol that will be used to represent the knot in the project diagrams throughout the book.

Overhand Knot

This basic knot is used to reinforce other knots or tie multiple strands together.

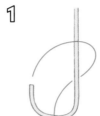

1

Wrap the cord end around itself and then through the loop it forms, as indicated by the arrow above.

2

Pull the cord end to tighten the knot.

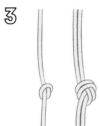

3

Completed overhand knot. You can also use this same technique to make a knot with multiple strands of cord.

Square Knot

Composed of two overhand knots turned in opposite ways, a square knot flattens when pulled tight.

1

Pass the left (blue) cord over, under, and then over the right (yellow) cord.

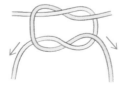

2

Next, cross the right (yellow) cord over the left (blue) cord, passing the ends of each cord through the loop formed by the other.

3

Pull the cord ends to tighten the knot.

Slip Knot

A slip knot is used to collect multiple strands of cord. Only one strand does the tying, so the knot is always small, even if there are several strands of cord being secured. Beware, a slip knot can be easily loosened.

Wrap one strand of cord around the others and itself, then insert the cord end through the loop.

Pull the cord end to tighten the knot.

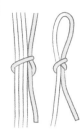

Completed slip knot. You can use this same technique to make a slip knot using a single strand of cord.

Gathering Knot

Use this technique to secure a bundle of cords that need to be grouped together.

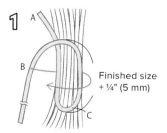

Finished size + ¼" (5 mm)

Fold the working cord over the bundle you want to group together. Wrap end B around the bundle from top to bottom, stopping ¼" (5 mm) above folded loop C.

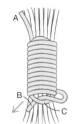

Insert end B through folded loop C.

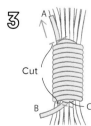

Cut

Pull end A upward to draw loop C under the wraps until it is hidden. Trim ends A and B, then tuck them under the coils to hide the loose ends.

Cross Knot

This knot features a square shape on the right side and a cross shape on the wrong side, making it a good luck symbol.

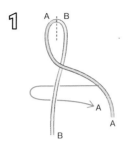

1 Fold the cord in half. Cross A over B. Make a small loop with A and bring it under B.

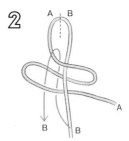

2 Bring B under A and then through the top and left loops.

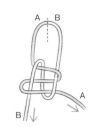

3 Pull cord ends A and B to tighten the knot and adjust the shape.

Three Strand Braid

This is the most popular type of braid. In fact, this style of braid is commonly used on hair. Alternately cross the outer strands over the center strand to form this braid.

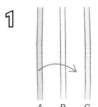

1 Cross A over B.

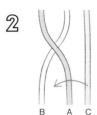

2 Cross C over A.

3 Continue crossing the left and right outer cords over the center cord, tightening the braid as you work.

Six Strand Braid

Use this technique to create a wider braid.

1

A BD C E F

Cross C over D. Next, cross D over B and E over C.

2

A D BE C F

Cross B over E.

3

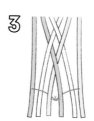

A D E B C F

Bring A and F to the center, passing them over and then under, as indicated by the arrows.

4

D E A F B C

Cross A over F. Repeat steps 3 and 4, tightening the braid as you work.

Alternating Half Hitch Knot

With this method, you'll alternately wrap the working cord and filler cord around each other.

1

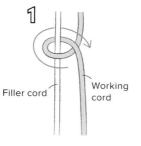

Filler cord
Working cord

Wrap the working cord around the filler cord in a clockwise direction.

2

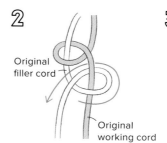

Original filler cord

Original working cord

Next, wrap the filler cord around the working cord in a counterclockwise direction.

3

One alternating half hitch knot is now complete. Repeat this process until the work reaches desired length.

Square Knot (Left & Right Facing)

With this technique, you'll make a basic square knot around filler cords.

Left facing   Right facing

Note *Following these steps will create a left facing square knot. To create a right facing square knot, simply start by bending B over the filler cords first. You can tell which type of square knot you've made by the vertical bar—it's on the left side for a left facing square knot and the right side for a right facing square knot. Both types are visible in the photo above.*

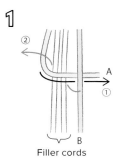

1

Bend A over the filler cords (①). Bring B under the filler cords and insert it through the loop created by A (②).

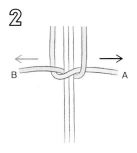

2

Pull A and B horizontally to tighten. Half of one square knot is now complete.

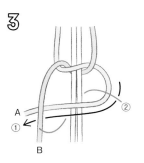

3

Bend A over the filler cords (①). Bring B under the filler cords and insert it through the loop created by A (②).

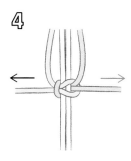

4

Pull A and B horizontally to tighten. One square knot is now complete.

Berry Knot

Roll continuous square knots into a ball to create a popcorn-shaped knot. Change the number of square knots to change the size of the berry knot. The number inside the symbol indicates how many square knots are used.

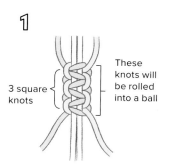

1

3 square knots

These knots will be rolled into a ball

Make the specified number of square knots.

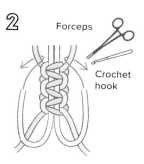

2

Forceps

Crochet hook

Insert the filler cord ends through the loops created by the working cords, as indicated by the red arrows. Use a crochet hook or forceps if necessary.

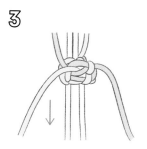

3

Pull the filler cords downward. This will cause the knots to roll into a ball.

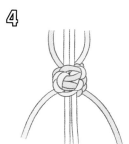

4

Make one square knot underneath the ball to hold it in place.

Spiral Knot

This knot is created when just half of the square knot is tied repeatedly. Tie half of a left facing square knot to form a spiral that twists from left to right or half of a right facing square knot to form a spiral that twists from right to left.

Left facing

Right facing

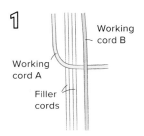

Bend A over the filler cords, then arrange B on top.

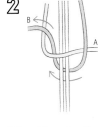

Bring B under the filler cords and insert it through the loop created by B.

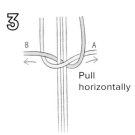

Pull A and B horizontally to tighten. One half square knot is now complete.

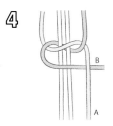

Bend B over the filler cords, then arrange A on top.

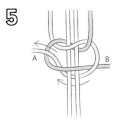

Bring A under the filler cords and insert it through the loop created by B.

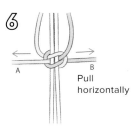

Pull A and B horizontally to tighten. Two half square knots are now complete.

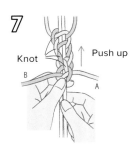

Repeat steps 1-6 until you reach the desired length. Push the knots upward to tighten as necessary.

Note *As the spiral turns, the left and right working cords will naturally switch positions and the work will revolve. The knot is reversible, so you don't have to worry about changing your knotting process.*

Crown Knot

This technique is commonly used as a decorative finish. The cords appear to be intertwined in a complex manner, but you are basically creating a braided ring.

1

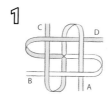

Make a loop with each cord, then insert each cord end through the adjacent loop, working in a clockwise direction.

2

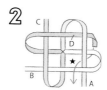

Insert D through the ★ area from back to front.

3

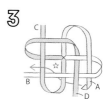

Insert A through the ☆ area from back to front.

4

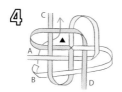

Insert B through the ▲ area from back to front.

5

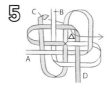

Insert C through the △ area from back to front.

6

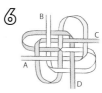

Make sure that all cords face upward as they exit the center point.

7

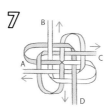

Pull the cord ends in the directions indicated by the arrows to tighten the knot.

8

Use an awl to gently pull the cord segments one at a time to tighten the knot.

9

Pull the cord ends up and down to adjust the shape of the knot.

Horizontal Clove Hitch

This technique involves wrapping each working cord around a horizontal filler cord twice to make tidy rows of knots.

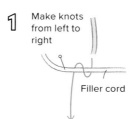

1 Make knots from left to right

Filler cord

Pin a horizontal filler cord to the board so it is taut. Wrap a vertical working cord around the filler cord by bringing it under, over, and then back under the filler cord.

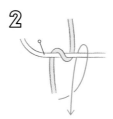

2 Next, wrap the working cord around the filler cord again, as indicated by the arrow.

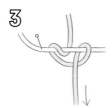

3 Pull the cord end downward to tighten.

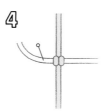

4 One horizontal clove hitch knot is now complete.

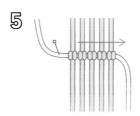

5 Follow the same process used in steps 1-3 to add additional working cords to the filler cord.

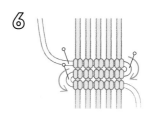

6 When the first row is complete, pin the filler cord in place and then bend it back across the work in the opposite direction. Work the next row of horizontal clove hitch knots from right to left, as shown in the diagram above. Position the second row of knots as close to the first as possible. Continue working rows back and forth.

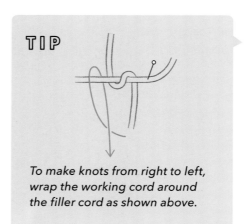

TIP

To make knots from right to left, wrap the working cord around the filler cord as shown above.

Vertical Clove Hitch

With the vertical clove hitch, you'll wrap a horizontal working cord around each vertical filler cord twice.

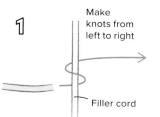

1 Pin a vertical filler cord to the board so it is taut. Starting from the left, wrap a horizontal working cord around the filler cord by bringing it under, over, and then back under the filler cord.

2 Next, wrap the working cord around the filler cord again as indicated by the arrow.

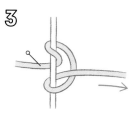

3 Pull the cord end to the right to tighten. One vertical clove hitch knot is now complete. Pin additional filler cords to the board and follow the same process used in steps 1-3 to knot the working cord around the filler cords.

Note *When the first row is complete, pin the working cord in place on the right edge of the filler cords, then work the next row from right to left, wrapping in the opposite direction.*

Diagonal Clove Hitch

With this variation, you'll work the horizontal clove hitch diagonally.

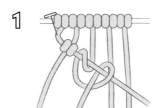

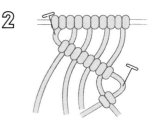

Use the first vertical cord as the filler cord and the remaining vertical cords as the working cords. Make horizontal clove hitch knots as shown on page 60, but arrange the knots in a diagonal line.

At the end of the row, bend the filler cord back across the work and reverse direction, wrapping in the opposite direction when knotting.

Reverse Horizontal Clove Hitch

With this knot, the reverse side of the horizontal clove hitch is visible on the right side of the work. It creates a cross pattern.

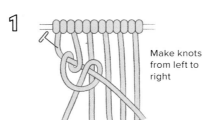

Make knots from left to right

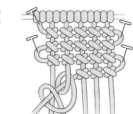

Use the first vertical cord as the filler cord and the remaining vertical cords as the working cords. Wrap the working cord over, under, and then over the filler cord first, then wrap it under and over again.

Continue in this manner until the first row is complete. Bend the filler cord back across the work and reverse direction, wrapping in the opposite direction when knotting. Continue working rows in alternate directions.

Enclosed Clove Hitch

Use this technique to conceal a vertical working cord that is not in use.

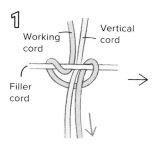

Working cord

Vertical cord

Filler cord

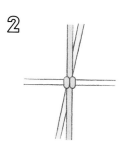

Insert the vertical cord in between the horizontal clove hitch before tightening.

The knot is complete.

Reverse Enclosed Clove Hitch

You can use the same process shown above to conceal a vertical cord when working a reverse clove hitch.

Step-by-Step Project Example

The following guide features step-by-step photos and instructions for making the Treasure Mesh Bag featured on page 20. Although these photos show the Treasure Mesh Bag, the same basic macramé techniques are used for several projects in the book. Refer to page 88 for more instructions on making the Treasure Mesh Bag.

Step 1: Make the Handles

The handles for this bag are made by working a continuous square knot pattern. For each handle, you'll start at the center and work to one end, then rotate the handle and work from the center to the other end. Repeat the process to make a second handle.

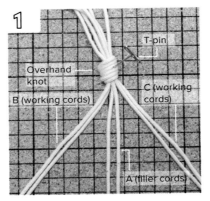

Arrange two filler cords (A) in the center with two working cords on each side (B and C). Align the cords at the center and temporarily secure with an overhand knot. Use a T-pin to secure the overhand knot to the board.

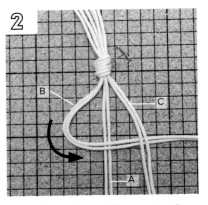

Bring B over A and then under C.

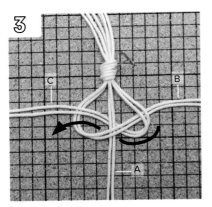

Bring C under A and then through the loop formed by B.

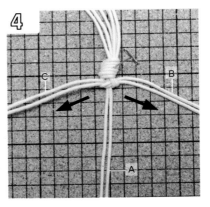

Pull working cords B and C sideways to tighten. Half of one square knot is now complete.

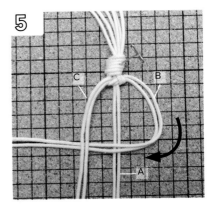

Next, bring B, which now on the right, over A and then under C.

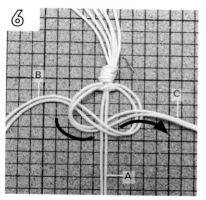

6

Bring C under A and then through the loop formed by B.

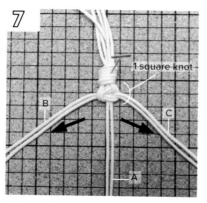

7

Pull working cords B and C sideways to tighten. One square knot is now complete.

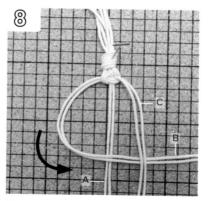

8

Next, you'll repeat the process shown in steps 2-4 again. Start by bringing B over A and under C.

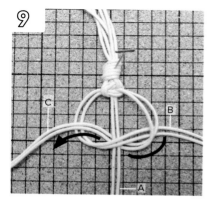

9

Bring C under A and then through the loop formed by B.

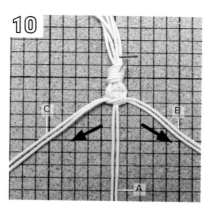

10

Pull working cords B and C sideways to tighten. One and a half square knots are now complete at this point.

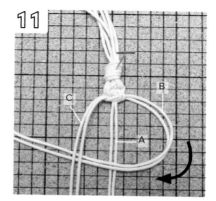

11

Next, you'll repeat the process shown in steps 5-7 again. Start by bringing B, which is now on the right, over A and under C.

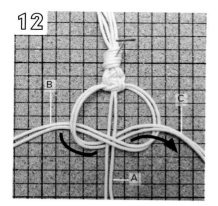

12

Bring C under A and through the loop formed by B.

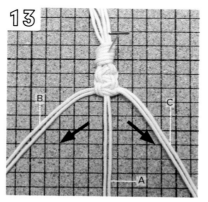

13

Pull working cords B and C sideways to tighten. Two square knots are now complete.

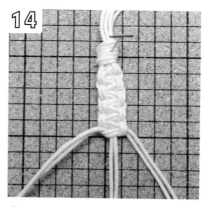

14

Continue this process to work square knots for 6¼" (16 cm), moving the position of the T-pin as necessary while you work.

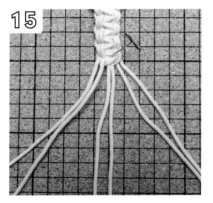

15

Once the square knots measure 6¼" (16 cm), untie the overhand knot from step 1, rotate the handle 180 degrees, and secure with a T-pin. Follow the same process to work square knots for another 6¼" (16 cm).

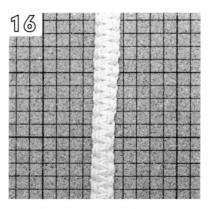

16

Completed view of the handle once square knots have been worked for another 6¼" (16 cm).

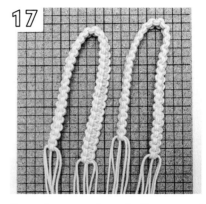

17

Repeat process to make the second handle.

Step 2: Make the Bag Body

MAKE THE TOP PORTION OF THE BAG BODY

Use the diagram on pages 90-91 as a reference to work a treasure mesh pattern for the top portion of the bag body. This treasure mesh pattern is composed of alternating square knots—it may look complex, but it's actually quite simple to make!

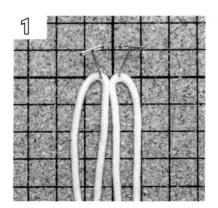

1

Fold two 47¼" (120 cm) pieces of cord in half and pin the centers to the board so the cords are side by side.

2

Make a square knot using the two center cords as the filler cord.

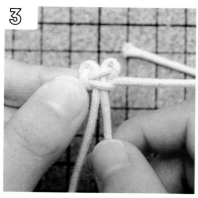

3

Pull the right filler cord to adjust the shape of the top right portion.

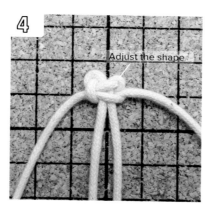

4

Completed view once the top right portion has been adjusted.

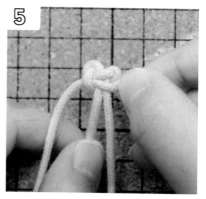

5

Pull the left filler cord to adjust the shape of the top left portion.

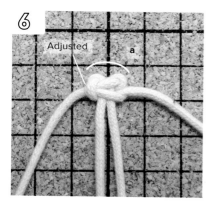

6

Completed view once the top left portion has been adjusted. This set of four cords will now be referred to as **a**.

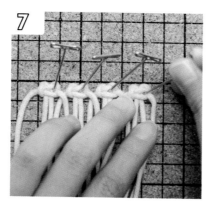

7

Make 36 **a** sets, arranging them side by side on the board.

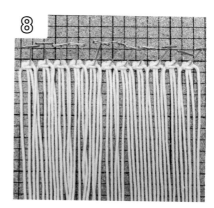

8

If you can't fit all 36 **a** sets on your board, line up as many as can fit comfortably and work in batches.

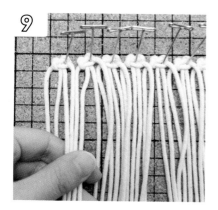

9

To make the first row, skip the first two cords, then group together the two rightmost cords from the first **a** set and the two leftmost cords from the second **a** set. Make a square knot using these four cords.

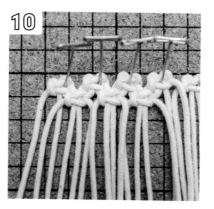

10

Repeat the process used in step 9 to continue making square knots using the cords from adjacent sets.

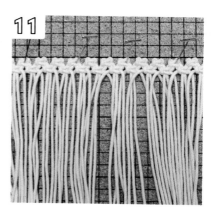

11

One row of the treasure mesh pattern is now complete (for the amount of **a** sets that can fit on the board).

Step-by-Step Project Example

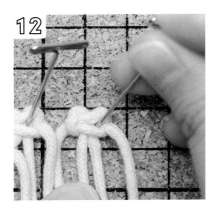

Unpin the work and move it over. Arrange the remaining **a** sets on the board next to the completed section and follow the same process to complete the first row of the treasure mesh pattern with the remaining **a** sets. Note that two cords at each end of the work remain untied.

To make the second row of the treasure mesh pattern, leave the four outermost cords on each end untied and make square knots using four adjacent cords for each set. The photo above shows the work after the second row of the treasure mesh pattern is complete.

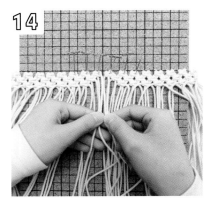

Wrap the work around the board and align the two ends. Group the two cords from each end of the first row.

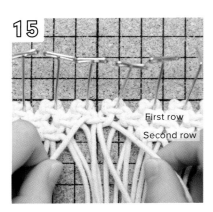

First row
Second row

Make a square knot using the four cords from step **14**. The ends of the work have now been joined together to create a tube. Next, take the strings that were left untied in the second row and make a square knot with each set of four cords.

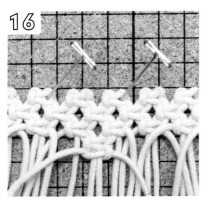

Take two cords each from adjacent sets and make 1.5 square knots.

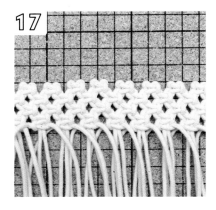

Repeat step **16** across the entire tube. The top portion of the bag body is now complete. It is a treasure mesh pattern composed of two rows of single alternating square knots and one row of 1.5 alternating square knots.

MAKE THE REST OF THE BAG BODY

You'll continue using the same technique to make the rest of the bag body, but this time, you'll use 1.5 square knots when working the treasure measure pattern. Use the diagram on pages 90-91 as a reference.

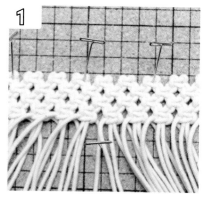

Insert a T-pin into the board ⅝" (1.5 cm) from the top portion of the bag body that was just completed.

TIP

How to Pin Macramé Securely

Insert T-pins into the board at the opposite angle to that which the cord will be pulled. It's also helpful to insert the pins through the knots rather than the cord.

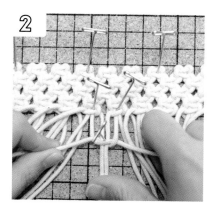

Insert a couple T-pins into the top portion of the bag body to hold the work in place. Make 1.5 square knots beneath the pin inserted in step 1. This will create a ⅝" (1.5 cm) space between the top portion of the bag body and the knot you just made.

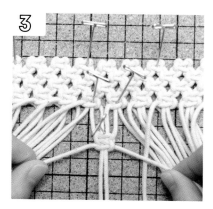

Carefully pull the cord ends to tighten the knots.

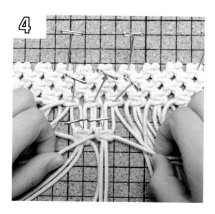

Continue making 1.5 square knots ⅝" (1.5 cm) from the top portion of the bag body.

Note *If you don't have enough pins, make a ⅝" (1.5 cm) wide cardboard spacer instead.*

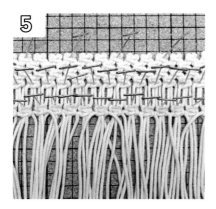

5

One row is now complete.

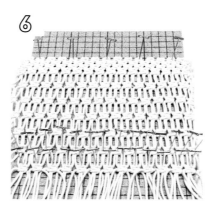

6

Follow this process to work a total of seven rows.

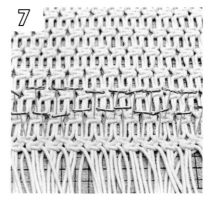

7

Next, work one row of square knots ⅝" (1.5 cm) from row 7. Work another row of alternating square knots directly below the first (do not leave any space).

MAKE THE BOTTOM

Once the bag body is complete, it's time to form the bottom of the bag and finish the cord ends.

1

Turn the bag body inside out.

2

Refer to the diagram on pages 90-91 to align cord ends noted by ♡ symbols. These cord ends will be positioned along the sides of the bag and will be used to create the gussets, or corners of the bag.

3

Make a square knot with the first set of cords.

4

Make a square knot with the next set of cords.

5

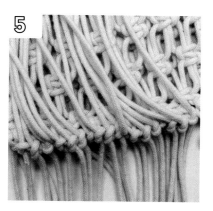

Next, align the cord ends noted by ☆ symbols. These will be positioned on opposite sides of the bag. Make square knots with corresponding sets of cords to form the bottom of the bag.

6

Once all the knots are made, use a bamboo skewer to apply glue to the cord ends and knots. Take care when applying the glue as you want to avoid excess glue seeping out onto the right side of the bag.

7

Once the glue is dry, trim the cord ends, leaving about ¾" (2 cm). Turn the bag right side out.

TIP

How to Finish Cord Ends with a Tapestry Needle

The finishing method shown here works well for the bottom of a bag, but if the area will be visible on the finished bag, such as on the handle, you'll want to use a different finishing method. Simply thread the cord ends onto a tapestry needle and weave under knots on the wrong side of the bag. If you are worried about the cord ends coming loose, apply a bit of glue.

Step 3: Attach the Handles

To finish the bag, you'll need to attach the handles to the body at the designated positions and finish the cord ends on the wrong side. If you don't have forceps, you can thread the cord ends onto a tapestry needle for finishing.

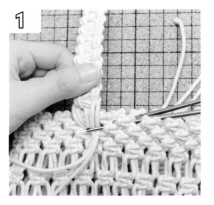

Align the handle ends with the bag body at the positions noted by the ▲☆◉ symbols in the diagram on pages 90-91. Use forceps to pull the cord ends through from the right side of the bag.

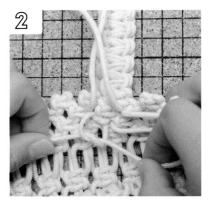

On the inside of the bag, tie a square knot with each set of two cords.

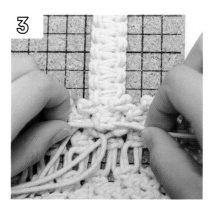

Make sure to pull the knots tight.

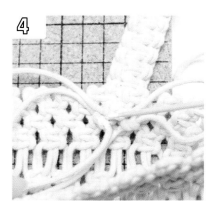

Use a bamboo skewer to apply glue to the cord ends and knots.

Once the glue dries, use forceps to pull the cord ends under an adjacent knot to prevent them from popping out.

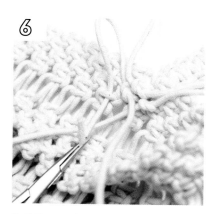

6

Pull the cord ends under the angled portions of adjacent square knots.

7

Trim the excess cord, leaving about ¼" (5 mm).

8

Turn the completed bag right side out.

How to Use This Book

This book was originally published in Japan, where macramé instructions are represented through the use of diagrams. Macramé diagrams contain all the information you'll need to construct the project, including where to start, which knots to use, and how many knots to make. The following guide explains how to read the macramé diagrams in this book.

STARTING POINT

Each macramé diagram will note the starting point and include an arrow indicating which direction to work.

Note *Several of the macramé diagrams are very large, so they are spread out across two pages. Work the diagram as a whole.*

SCHEMATIC NOTES

Macramé diagrams are two-dimensional representations of three-dimensional projects. They are basically what the bag would look like if it was flattened. You'll see notes indicating the sides, center, and other important points on each project.

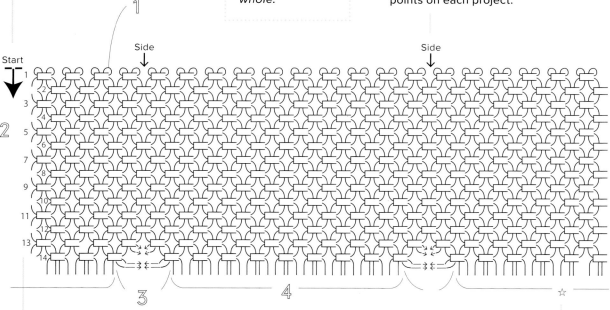

ROW NUMBER

The small numbers in the diagrams indicate the row numbers.

STEP NUMBER

The large numbers in the diagrams indicate step numbers. Each project will also include a written list of instructions that correspond to these numbers.

SYMBOLS

The diagrams will often contain symbols indicating sections of the bag that should be aligned when tying knots to form the bottom or corners of the bag.

project instructions ▷

01 · 02
Black & White Net Purses with Leather Handles

Photos on pages 10-13

MATERIALS

FOR 1

46 ft (14 m) of 2 mm black cotton cord

122 ft (37 m) of 3 mm black cotton cord

FOR 2

46 ft (14 m) of 2 mm white cotton cord

122 ft (37 m) of 3 mm white cotton cord

> Bag body working cords (3 mm):
> 67" (170 cm) x 16 pieces
> 63" (160 cm) x 6 pieces
>
> Strap A working cords (2 mm):
> 43¼" (110 cm) x 4 pieces
>
> Strap A filler cords (2 mm):
> 15¾" (40 cm) x 4 pieces
>
> Strap B working cords (2 mm):
> 51¼" (130 cm) x 4 pieces
>
> Strap B filler cords (2 mm):
> 19¾" (50 cm) x 4 pieces

FOR BOTH

Two 14" (36 cm) pieces of ⅝" (1.5 cm) wide leather tape

Four ⅜" (8 mm) diameter rivets

Four ¾" (1.8 cm) wide D-rings

½ yard (0.5 m) of lining fabric

Two 39½" (100 cm) pieces of 2 mm diameter leather cord

SYMBOL KEY

 Square Knot
▷ *page 56*

 Square Knot
▷ *page 52*

 Cross Knot
▷ *page 54*

FINISHED SIZE

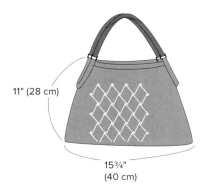

11" (28 cm)

15¾"
(40 cm)

MAKE THE HANDLES (MAKE 2)

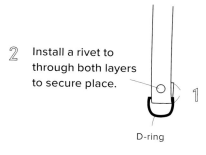

2 Install a rivet to through both layers to secure place.

D-ring

1 For each piece of leather tape, insert the ends through a D-ring and fold over ¾" (2 cm).

SEW THE BAG LINING

1 Cut a 17¾" x 31" (45 x 78 cm) rectangle of fabric for the lining. Fold in half with right sides together. Mark each side 5½" (14 cm) from the top. This will be the end of the opening for the drawstring.

2 Fold and press the top 5½" (14 cm) over ¼" (5 mm) twice and topstitch.

3 Sew the edges together below the mark using ⅜" (1 cm) seam allowance.

4 Fold and press the top of the bag over 1⅜" (3.5 cm) twice. Topstitch ¾" (2 cm) from the edge.

5 Turn right side out. Insert the leather cords through the casing in opposite directions and tie the ends together.

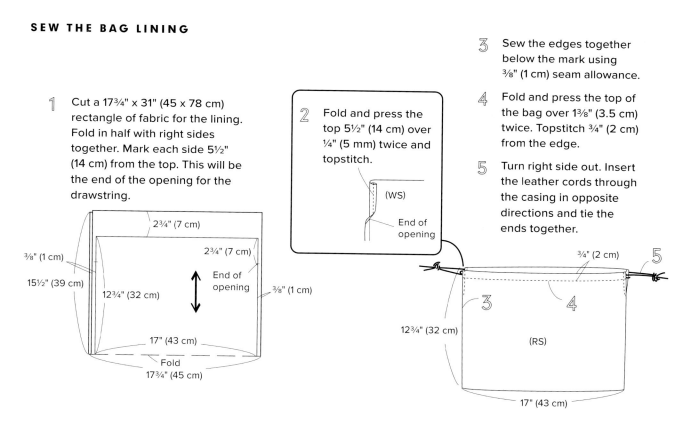

2¾" (7 cm)
2¾" (7 cm)
⅜" (1 cm)
15½" (39 cm)
12¾" (32 cm)
End of opening
⅜" (1 cm)
17" (43 cm)
Fold
17¾" (45 cm)

(WS)
End of opening

¾" (2 cm)
12¾" (32 cm)
(RS)
17" (43 cm)

MAKE THE BAG BODY

1. Make two each of Strap A and B. Align the cords at the center and work square knots from the center outward, as indicated by the arrows.

2. Insert the A cord ends through the B knots as indicated by the pink circles. Make square knots on the wrong side to secure.

3. Insert the 67" (170 cm) working cords through the side loops of the square knots of Strap A, following the placement noted in the diagram.

4. For the areas noted with the ♡ symbol, insert three 63" (160 cm) working cords through the side loops of the square knots of Strap B, following the placement noted in the diagram.

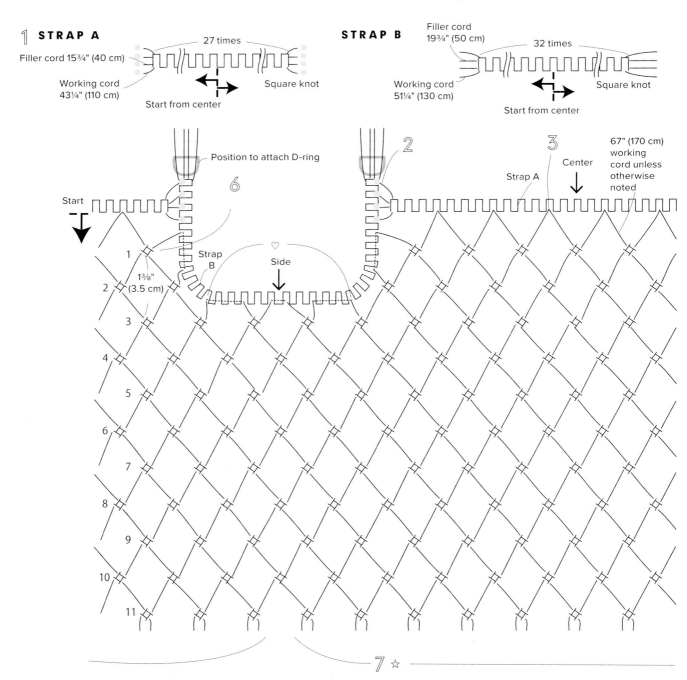

5 Use the same process to insert two 67" (170 cm) working cords through the side loops of the square knots of Strap B on each side, following the placement noted in the diagram.

6 Work 11 rows of cross knots with 1⅜" (3.5 cm) of vertical space between each row. Make sure to join the ends together to create a tube-shaped bag.

7 Turn the bag inside out. To form the bottom of the bag, make square knots with the opposite side of the bag where you see a ☆ symbol. Finish the cord ends by inserting them through the wrong side of the cross knots from row 11.

8 Insert the cord ends of Strap B through the D-rings and secure in place on the wrong side of the bag. Insert the lining into the bag.

Leather handle

11" (28 cm)

15¾" (40 cm)

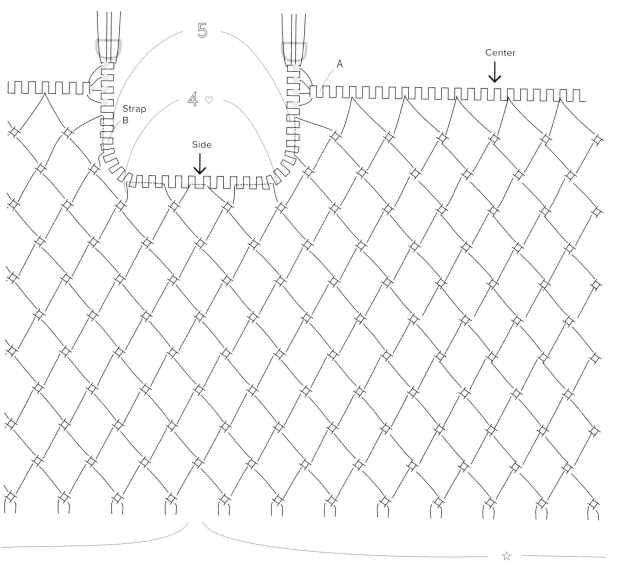

5

A

Center

Strap B

4 ♡

Side

Black & White Net Purses with Leather Handles

Cross-Body Drawstring Bag

Photo on page 14

MATERIALS

371 ft (113 m) of 3 mm natural cotton cord

Bag body working cords:
78¾" (200 cm) x 48 pieces
Bag body filler cords:
31½" (80 cm) x 5 pieces
Strap cords: 90½" (230 cm) x 3 pieces
Drawstring cords: 47¼" (120 cm) x 3 pieces
Drawstring loop cords: 24" (60 cm) x 4 pieces

SYMBOL KEY

 Starting Method C
▷ *page 51*

 Horizontal Clove Hitch
▷ *page 60*

 Overhand Knot
▷ *page 52*

 Square Knot
▷ *page 56*

 Enclosed Clove Hitch
▷ *page 63*

 Square Knot
▷ *page 52*

 Three Strand Braid
▷ *page 54*

FINISHED SIZE

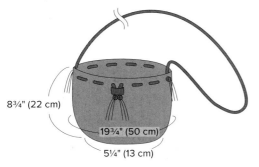

8¾" (22 cm)

19¾" (50 cm)

5¼" (13 cm)

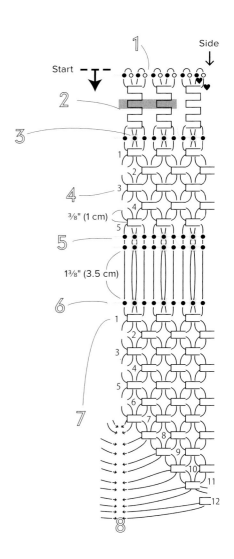

MAKE THE BAG BODY

1. Fold the 48 working cords in half at the center and attach one of the filler cords using starting method C. At the side of the bag, overlap the ends of the filler cord to form a loop and secure in place when attaching 4 of the working cords to the overlapped filler cords.

2. Make 3.5 square knots with adjacent sets of working cords. Make sure to join the ends together to create a tube-shaped bag.

3. Knot 1 row of horizontal clove hitch and enclosed clove hitch, overlapping the ends of the filler cord to form a loop.

4. Knot 5 rows of single alternating square knots to form a treasure mesh pattern.

5. Knot 2 rows of horizontal clove hitch and enclosed clove hitch, overlapping the ends of the filler cord to form a loop.

6. Leave a 1⅜" (3.5 cm) vertical space, and then work 1 row of horizontal clove hitch and enclosed clove hitch, overlapping the ends of the filler cord to form a loop.

7. Knot 12 rows of single alternating square knots to form a treasure mesh pattern. Start decreasing the number of knots at row 7.

8. Turn the bag inside out. Make square knots, connecting the cord ends as indicated by the arrows, to form the bottom of the bag. Finish the cord ends as shown on page 71.

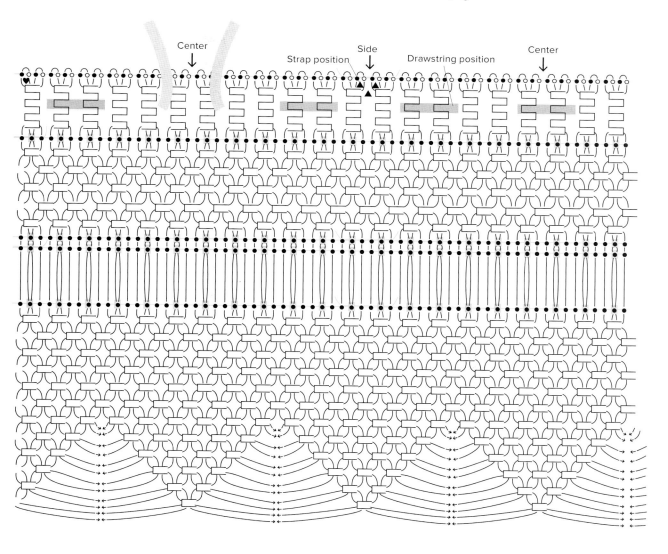

Center   Strap position   Side   Drawstring position   Center

MAKE THE STRAP

Use the 3 strap cords to work a three strand braid for 51¼" (130 cm), leaving 8" (20 cm) unbraided at each end. Insert the cord ends through the bag body at the positions noted by the ♥ and ▲ symbols in the diagram on pages 80-81 (insert from right side to wrong side). Make overhand knots with all 3 cords to secure the strap in place. Trim the excess cord, leaving 6" (15 cm) at each end.

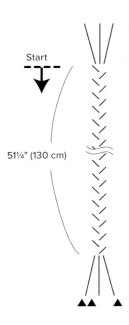

Start

51¼" (130 cm)

▲▲　▲

MAKE THE DRAWSTRING

Make an overhand knot with the 3 drawstring cords, leaving 6" (15 cm) at the top. Work a three strand braid for 21¾" (55 cm). Make another overhand knot at the end, and then trim the excess cord, leaving 6" (15 cm). Weave the drawstring through the bag body following the placement noted in the diagram on pages 80-81.

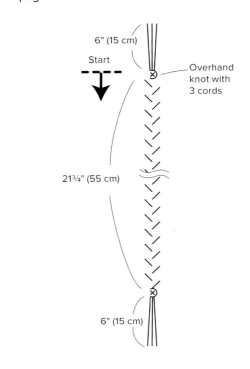

6" (15 cm)

Start

Overhand knot with 3 cords

21¾" (55 cm)

6" (15 cm)

MAKE THE DRAWSTRING LOOP

Fold the drawstring loop cords in half at the center. Work 7 rows of single alternating square knots to form a treasure mesh pattern. Wrap this piece around the two drawstring ends, forming a ring. Secure the ring in place by inserting the filler cords through the loops of the knots from the first row, then make a square knot with the cord ends.

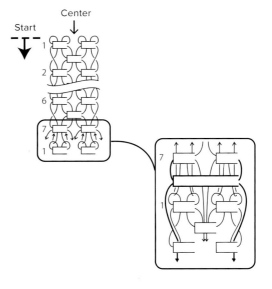

Start

Center

04

Diagonal Clove Hitch Clutch

Photo on page 16

MATERIALS

371 ft (113 m) of 2 mm yellow cotton cord

- Working cords: 55" (140 cm) x 80 pieces
- Filler cord: 27½" (70 cm) x 1 piece

FINISHED SIZE

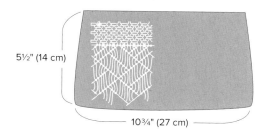

5½" (14 cm)

10¾" (27 cm)

SYMBOL KEY

 Square Knot
▷ *page 56*

 Diagonal Clove Hitch
▷ *page 62*

 Reverse Enclosed Clove Hitch
▷ *page 63*

 Square Knot
▷ *page 52*

 Reverse Horizontal Clove Hitch
▷ *page 62*

MAKE THE BAG BODY

1. Fold the 80 working cords in half at the center. Align in sets of two, so there are 40 sets total. Make 1 square knot with each set.

2. Knot 7 rows of single alternating square knots to form a treasure mesh pattern. Make sure to join the ends together to create a tube-shaped bag.

3. Knot 1 row of horizontal clove hitch and reverse enclosed clove hitch, overlapping the ends of the filler cord to form a loop.

4. Work diagonal clove hitch following the diagram.

5. Knot 3 rows of single alternating square knots to form a treasure mesh pattern. Decrease the number of knots starting at row 2.

6. Turn the bag inside out. Create the gussets by making square knots where you see a ♡ symbol.

7. To form the bottom of the bag, make square knots with the opposite side of the bag where you see a ☆ symbol. Finish the cord ends as shown on page 71.

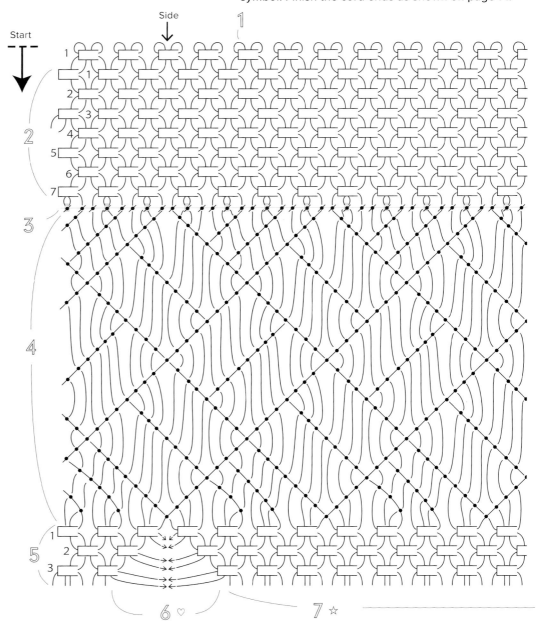

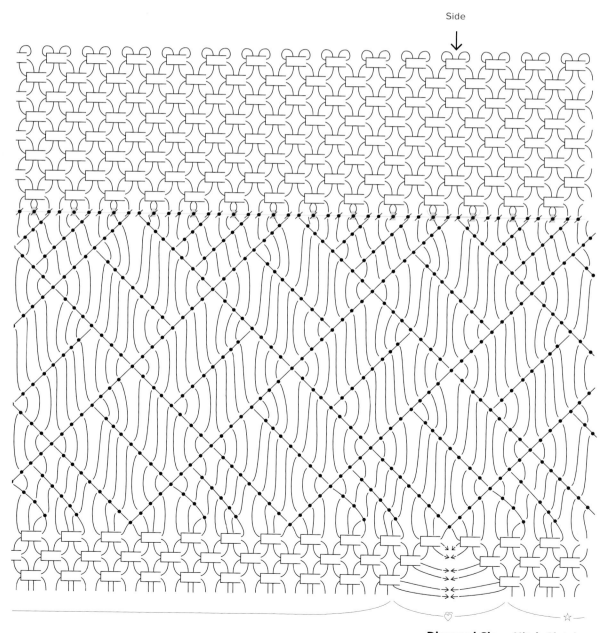

Side

Diagonal Clove Hitch Clutch

05
Popcorn Purse
Photo on page 18

MATERIALS

384 ft (117 m) of 3 mm dark red cotton cord

　Working cords: 94½" (240 cm) x 32 pieces

　Additional cords: 94½" (240 cm) x 16 pieces

　Filler cords: 23¾" (60 cm) x 2 pieces

One set of 3¾" x 6¼" (9.5 x 15.5 cm) wooden handles

SYMBOL KEY

 Starting Method A
▷ *page 50*

 Horizontal Clove Hitch
▷ *page 60*

 Diagonal Clove Hitch
▷ *page 62*

 Square Knot
▷ *page 52*

 Square Knot
▷ *page 56*

 Enclosed Clove Hitch
▷ *page 63*

 Berry Knot
▷ *page 57*

FINISHED SIZE

9½" (24 cm)

8" (20 cm)

MAKE THE BAG BODY

1　Attach 16 working cords to each handle using starting method A. Make 1 row of square knots using adjacent sets of working cords.

2　Fold the additional cords in half at the center and add them as noted in the diagram. Knot 4 rows of single alternating square knots to form a treasure mesh pattern. Do not leave any gaps between the rows.

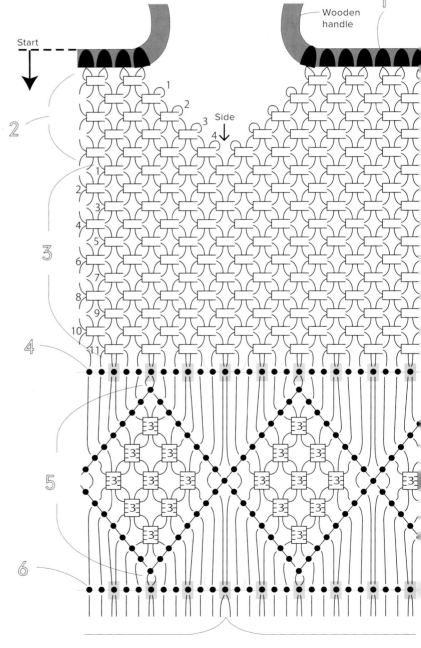

3 Knot an additional 11 rows of single alternating square knots to form a treasure mesh pattern. Make sure to join the ends together to create a tube-shaped bag.

4 Knot 1 row of horizontal clove hitch and enclosed clove hitch, overlapping the ends of the filler cord to form a loop.

5 Knot treasure mesh pattern with diagonal clove hitch and berry knots, as noted in the diagram.

6 Repeat step 4.

7 Turn the bag inside out. To form the bottom of the bag, make square knots with the opposite side of the bag where you see a ☆ symbol. Finish the cord ends as shown on page 71.

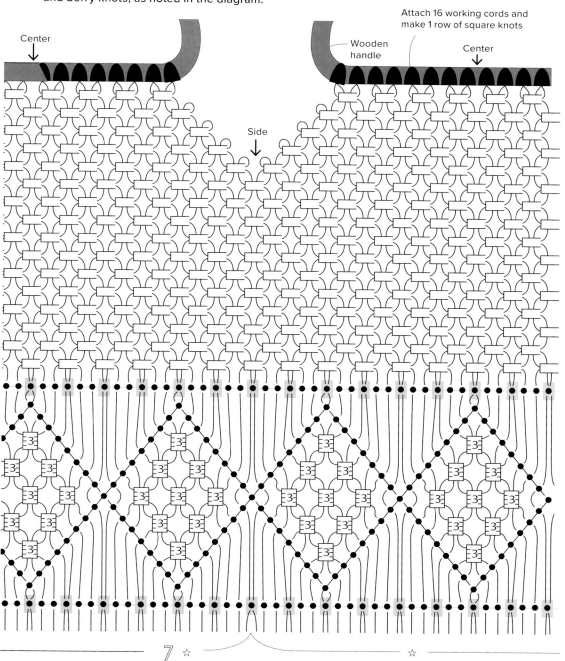

Center

Attach 16 working cords and make 1 row of square knots

Wooden handle

Center

Side

7 ☆   ☆

Treasure Mesh Bag

Photo on page 20

MATERIALS

381 ft (116 m) of 2 mm white cotton cord

> Bag body cords: 47¼" (120 cm) x 72 pieces
> Handle cord A: 25½" (65 cm) x 4 pieces
> Handle cord B: 78¾" (200 cm) x 4 pieces
> Handle cord C: 78¾" (200 cm) x 4 pieces

Refer to page 64 for step-by-step photos showing how to make this project from start to finish.

SYMBOL KEY

Overhand Knot
page 52

Square Knot
▷ *page 56*

Square Knot
▷ *page 52*

FINISHED SIZE

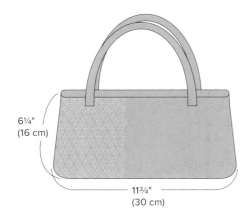

6¼"
(16 cm)

11¾"
(30 cm)

MAKE THE HANDLES (MAKE 2)

1   Arrange two pieces of handle cord A, two pieces of handle cord B, and two pieces of handle cord C as shown below. Align the cords at the center and temporarily secure with an overhand knot.

2   Starting at the center, work square knots for 6¼" (16 cm) using the two pieces of handle cord A as the filler cords and the pieces of handle cord B and C as the working cords. Rotate the handle 180 degrees, untie the overhand knot, and work square knots for another 6¼" (16 cm).

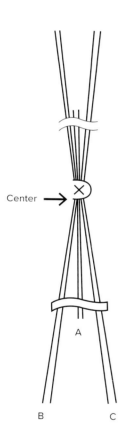

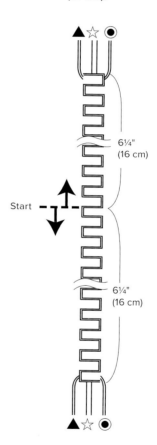

MAKE THE BAG BODY

1. Fold 2 pieces of bag body cord in half at the center. Arrange side by side and use this set to make one square knot. Repeat for a total of 36 sets.

2. Knot 2 rows of single alternating square knots to form a treasure mesh pattern. Make sure to join the ends together to create a tube-shaped bag.

3. Knot 7 rows of 1.5 alternating square knots to form a treasure mesh pattern, leaving ⅝" (1.5 cm) space between each row.

4. Leave ⅝" (1.5 cm) space, and knot 2 rows of single alternating square knots to form a treasure mesh pattern

5. Turn the bag inside out. Create the gussets by making square knots where you see a ♡ symbol. Finish the cord ends as shown on page 71.

6. To form the bottom of the bag, make square knots with the opposite side of the bag where you see a ☆ symbol. Finish the cord ends as shown on page 71.

7. Insert the handle cords through the right side of the bag body at the positions noted by the symbols (there should be 2 cords for each symbol). Use the cords to make square knots on the wrong side of the bag and secure with glue.

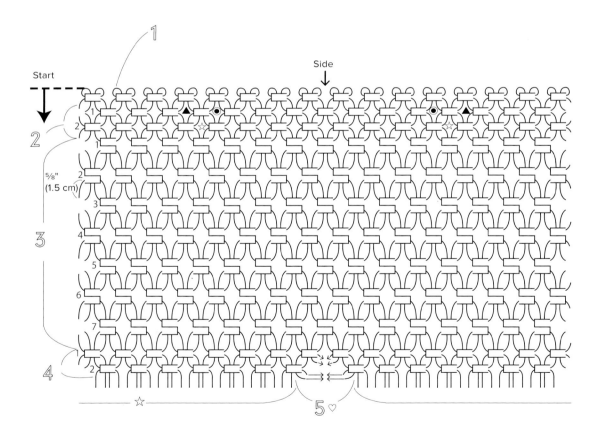

Center   7   Side   Center

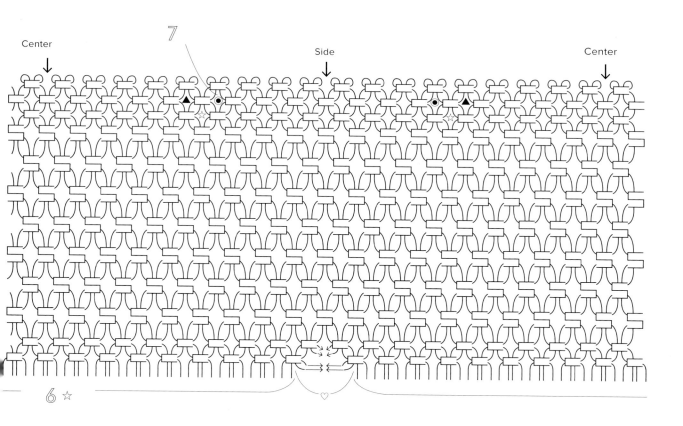

6 ☆

07
Net Bag with Wooden Handles

Photo on page 22

MATERIALS

381 ft (116 m) of 2 mm natural jute/bamboo cord

{ Working cords: 63" (160 cm) x 72 pieces

One set of 6¼" x 6¼" (16 x 15.5 cm) wooden handles

MAKE THE BAG BODY

1. Attach 36 working cords to each wooden handle using starting method A.

2. Make 10 left facing spiral knots using adjacent sets of working cords.

3. Knot 2 rows of 5 left facing alternating spiral knots to form a treasure mesh pattern.

4. Knot 6 rows of 1.5 alternating square knots to form a treasure mesh pattern, leaving a ⅝" (1.5 cm) gap between each row. Make sure to join the ends together to create a tube-shaped bag.

5. Knot another 4 rows of 1.5 alternating square knots to form a treasure mesh pattern, leaving a ¾" (2 cm) gap between each row.

6. Turn the bag inside out. To form the bottom of the bag, make square knots with the opposite side of the bag where you see a ☆ symbol.

7. Finish the cord ends by inserting them through the wrong side of the square knots from row 4.

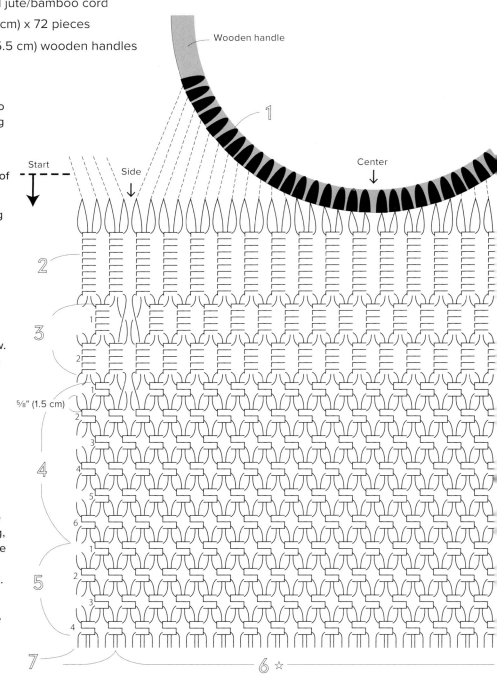

Wooden handle

Start

Side

Center

⅝" (1.5 cm)

SYMBOL KEY

Starting Method A
▷ page 50

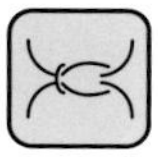

Square Knot
▷ page 52

Spiral Knot
▷ page 58

Square Knot
▷ page 56

FINISHED SIZE

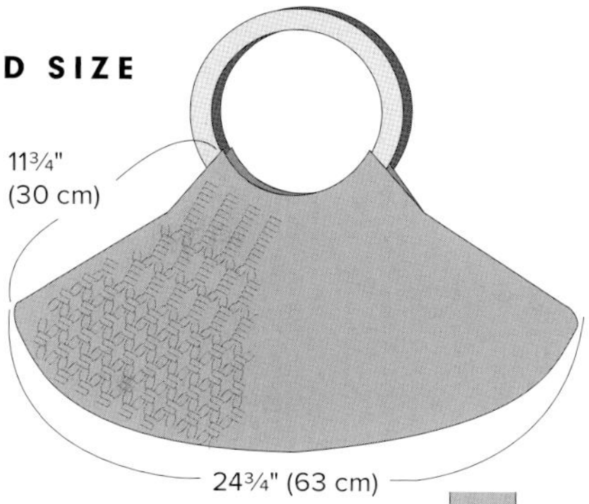

11¾"
(30 cm)

24¾" (63 cm)

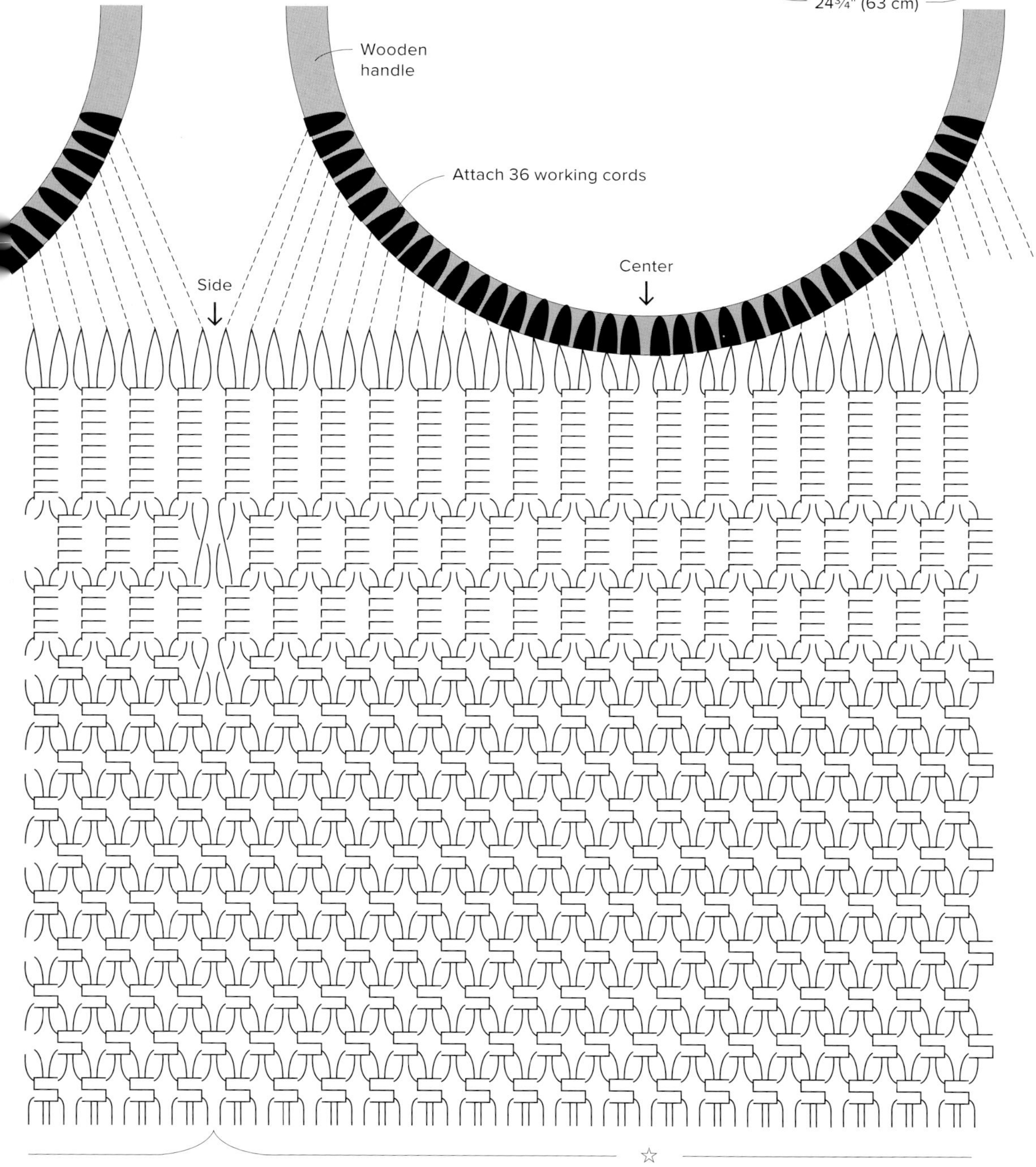

Wooden
handle

Attach 36 working cords

Side

Center

Net Bag with Wooden Handles

93

08
Mod Net Purse

Photo on page 24

MATERIALS

262½ ft (80 m) of 1.8 mm
natural hemp cord

> Working cords: 78¾"
> (200 cm) x 40 pieces

One set of 4¼" (11 cm) inner
diameter ivory plastic handles

SYMBOL KEY

Square Knot
▷ *page 56*

Square Knot
▷ *page 52*

Starting Method D
▷ *page 51*

FINISHED DIAGRAM

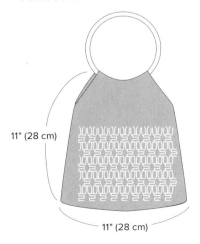

11" (28 cm)

11" (28 cm)

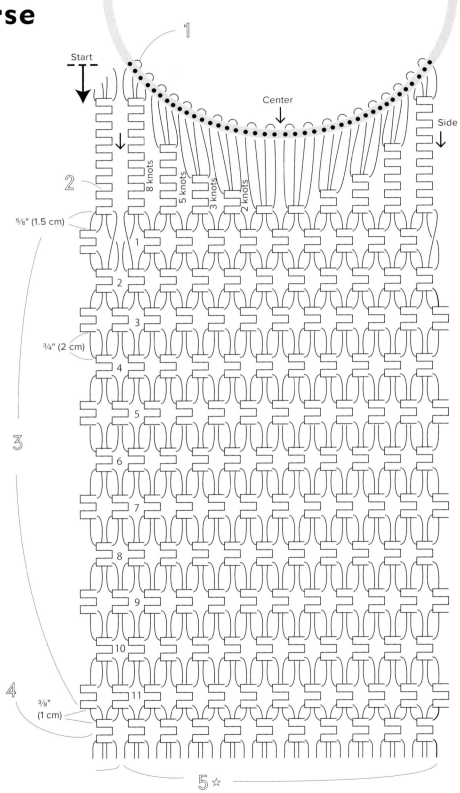

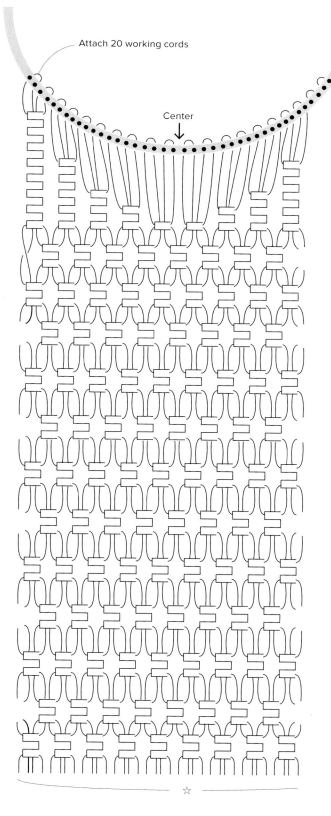

Attach 20 working cords

Center

MAKE THE BAG BODY

1   Attach 20 working cords to each handle using starting method D.

2   Use adjacent sets of working cords to make the specified number of square knots.

3   Knot 11 rows of double alternating square knots to form a treasure mesh pattern, leaving ¾" (2 cm) between each row. Make sure to join the ends together to create a tube-shaped bag.

4   Leave a ⅜" (1 cm) gap, then knot one row of double square knots using adjacent sets of working cords.

5   Turn the bag inside out. To form the bottom of the bag, make square knots with the opposite side of the bag where you see a ☆ symbol. Finish the cord ends by inserting them through the wrong side of the square knots from step 4.

Nylon Market Tote

Photo on page 26

MATERIALS

394 ft (120 m) of 2.5 mm black nylon cord

Filler cord A: 59" (150 cm) x 2 pieces

Working cord A: 59¼ ft (18 m) x 1 piece

Filler cord B: 9¾" (25 cm) x 4 pieces

Working cord B: 59" (150 cm) x 2 pieces

Bag body working cords: 71" (180 cm) x 44 pieces

SYMBOL KEY

 Vertical Clove Hitch
▷ *page 61*

 Square Knot
▷ *page 52*

 Square Knot
▷ *page 56*

How to Attach the Cords (Steps 2 & 3)

Insert the cord through the loop, and fold in half at the center

FINISHED DIAGRAM

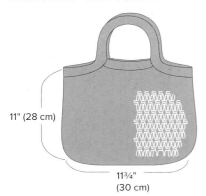

11" (28 cm)

11¾" (30 cm)

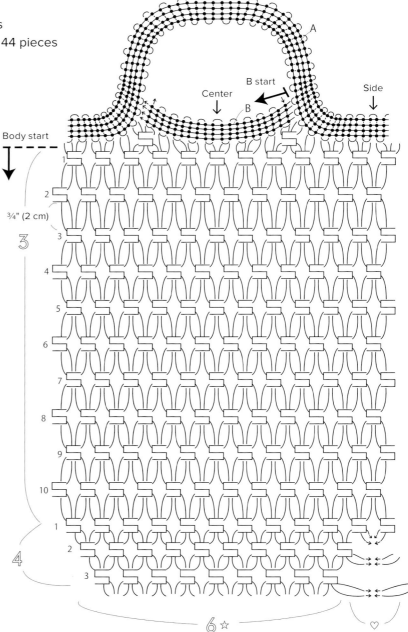

MAKE THE HANDLES & BAG BODY

1. Fold the two A filler cords in half and knot 144 rows of 4 vertical clove hitch knots using working cord A. Connect the beginning and end of the filler cords to make a loop (refer to the diagram below).

2. Fold two B filler cords in half and attach to A (refer to the diagram on the opposite page). Knot 20 rows of vertical clove hitch using one working cord B. Finish the cord ends by inserting through A (refer to the diagram on the opposite page). Repeat for the other handle.

3. Attach the bag body working cords to A and B (refer to the diagram on the opposite page). Knot 10 rows of 1.5 alternating square knots to form a treasure mesh pattern, leaving ¾" (2 cm) between rows. Make sure to join the ends together to create a tube-shaped bag.

4. Knot 3 rows of 1.5 alternating square knots to form a treasure mesh pattern without leaving any gaps between rows.

5. Turn the bag inside out. Create the gussets by making square knots where you see a ♡ symbol.

6. To form the bottom of the bag, make square knots with the opposite side of the bag where you see a ☆ symbol. Finish the cord ends as shown on page 71.

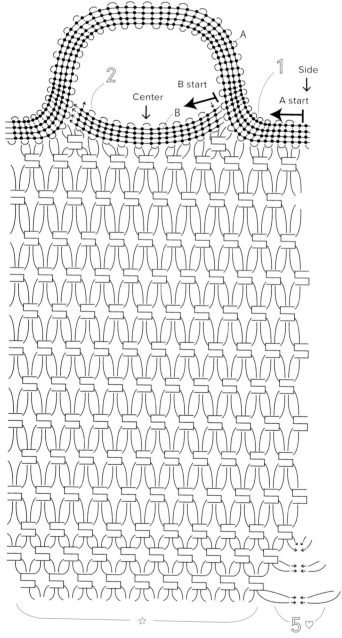

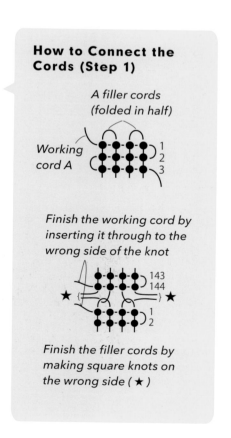

How to Connect the Cords (Step 1)

A filler cords (folded in half)

Working cord A

1
2
3

Finish the working cord by inserting it through to the wrong side of the knot

143
144

★ ★

1
2

Finish the filler cords by making square knots on the wrong side (★)

10
Solid Knit Pouch

Photo on page 30

MATERIALS

118 ft (36 m) of ¼" (7 mm) flat blue cotton yarn

⟨ Working cord: 35½" (90 cm) x 40 pieces

One ¾" (2 cm) magnetic button

SYMBOL KEY

Square Knot
▷ *page 56*

Square Knot
▷ *page 52*

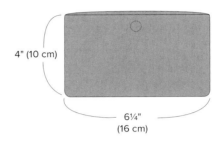

4" (10 cm)

6¼"
(16 cm)

MAKE THE BAG BODY

1. Fold the 40 working cords in half at the center. Align in sets of two, so there are 20 sets total. Make 1 square knot with each set.

2. Knot 13 rows of single alternating square knots to form a treasure mesh pattern. Make sure to join the ends together to create a tube-shaped bag.

3. Turn the bag inside out. Create the gussets by making square knots where you see a ♡ symbol.

4. To form the bottom of the bag, make square knots with the opposite side of the bag where you see a ☆ symbol. Finish the cord ends as shown on page 71.

5. Sew the magnetic button components to the inside of the pouch at the center.

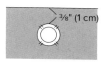

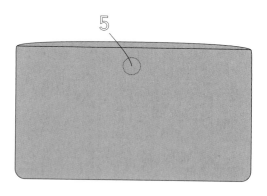

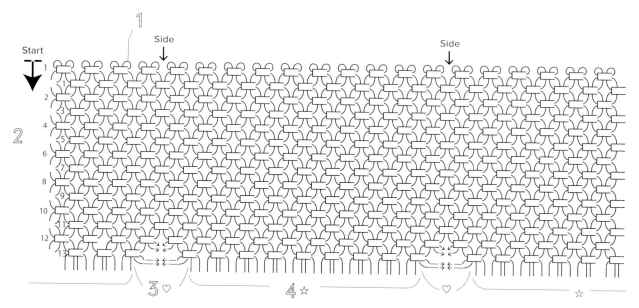

11
Striped Knit Pouch

Photo on page 31

MATERIALS

Color A: 73 ft (22 m) of ¼" (7 mm) flat blue cotton yarn

Color B: 50 ft (15 m) of ¼" (7 mm) flat dark blue cotton yarn

{ Working cord A: 35½" (90 cm) x 24 pieces
{ Working cord B: 35½" (90 cm) x 16 pieces

One ¾" (2 cm) magnetic button

SYMBOL KEY

 Square Knot
▷ *page 56*

 Square Knot
▷ *page 52*

FINISHED DIAGRAM

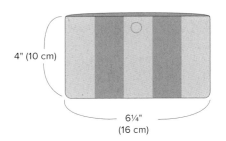

4" (10 cm)

6¼"
(16 cm)

MAKE THE BAG BODY

1   Fold the 40 working cords in half at the center (24 pieces of A and 16 pieces of B). Align in sets of two, so there are 20 sets total (refer to the diagram below for color placement). Make 1 square knot with each set.

2   Knot 13 rows of single alternating square knots to form a treasure mesh pattern. Make sure to join the ends together to create a tube-shaped bag.

3   Turn the bag inside out. Create the gussets by making square knots where you see a ♡ symbol.

4   To form the bottom of the bag, make square knots with the opposite side of the bag where you see a ☆ symbol. Finish the cord ends as shown on page 71.

5   Sew the magnetic button components to the inside of the pouch at the center.

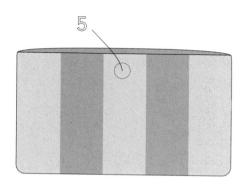

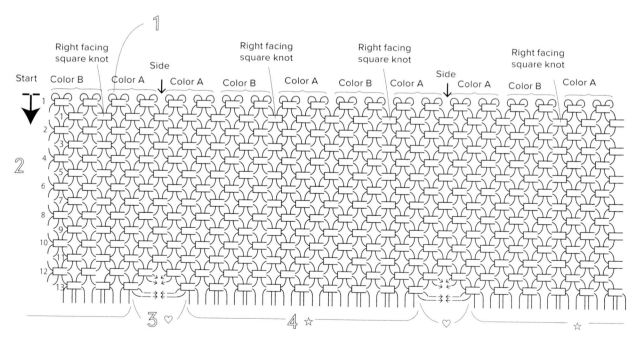

12
White Diamond Tassel Clutch

Photo on page 32

MATERIALS

308½ ft (94 m) of 2 mm white cotton cord

~ Working cords: 55" (140 cm) x 64 pieces
~ Filler cords: 19¾" (50 cm) x 2 pieces
~ Tassel cords: 98½" (250 cm) x 1 piece
~ 9¾" (25 cm) x 2 pieces

One 9" (22 cm) zipper

SYMBOL KEY

 Starting Method C
▷ *page 51*

 Diagonal Clove Hitch
▷ *page 62*

Square Knot
▷ *page 56*

 Square Knot
▷ *page 52*

Reverse Horizontal Clove Hitch
▷ *page 62*

 Enclosed Clove Hitch
▷ *page 63*

Horizontal Clove Hitch
▷ *page 60*

  Gathering Knot
▷ *page 53*

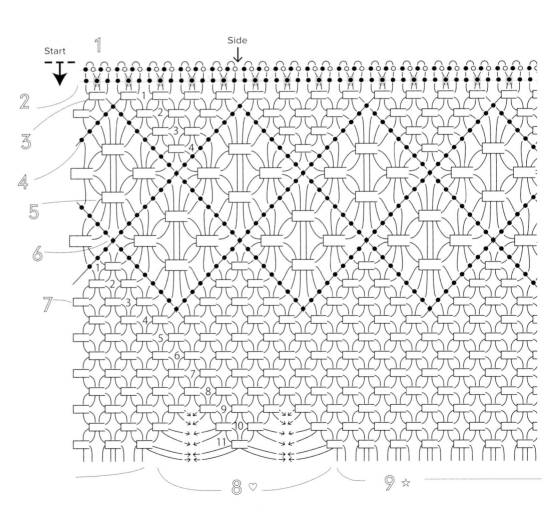

MAKE THE BAG BODY

1 Fold the 64 working cords in half at the center and attach to one of the filler cords using starting method C. Overlap the ends of the filler cord to form a loop and secure in place when attaching 4 of the working cords to the overlapped filler cord.

2 Knot 1 row of horizontal clove hitch and enclosed clove hitch, overlapping the ends of the filler cord to form a loop.

3 Knot 4 rows of single alternating square knots to form a treasure mesh pattern. Decrease the number of knots in each row. Make sure to join the ends together to create a tube-shaped bag.

4 Work diagonal clove hitch as noted in the diagram.

5 Make square knots using 4 strands as the filler cord.

6 Work reverse horizontal clove hitch as noted in the diagram.

7 Knot 11 rows of single alternating square knots to form a treasure mesh pattern. Decrease the number of knots starting at row 9.

8 Turn the bag inside out. Create the gussets by making square knots as indicated by the arrows where you see a ♡ symbol.

9 To form the bottom of the bag, make square knots with the opposite side of the bag where you see a ☆ symbol. Finish the cord ends as shown on page 71.

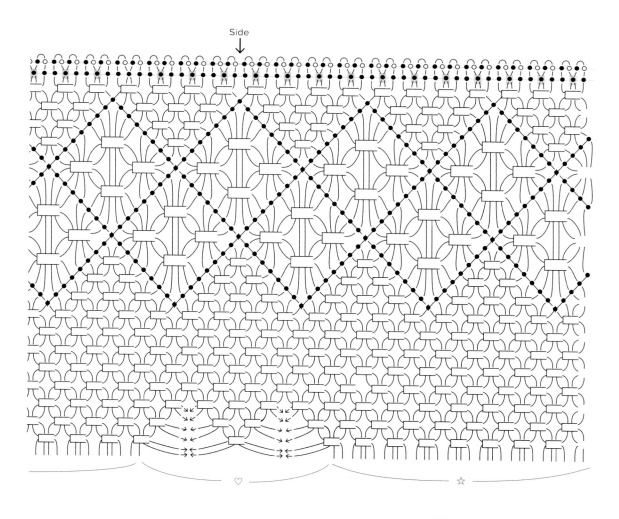

MAKE THE TASSEL

1 Wrap the 98½" (250 cm) tassel cord around an 8" (20 cm) tall piece of cardboard 5-6 times.

2 Use one of the 9¾" (25 cm) tassel cords to tie the wrapped bundle together at the center, and then remove the cardboard.

3 Use the remaining 9¾" (25 cm) tassel cord to tie a gathering knot around the bundle ⅝" (1.5 cm) from the top.

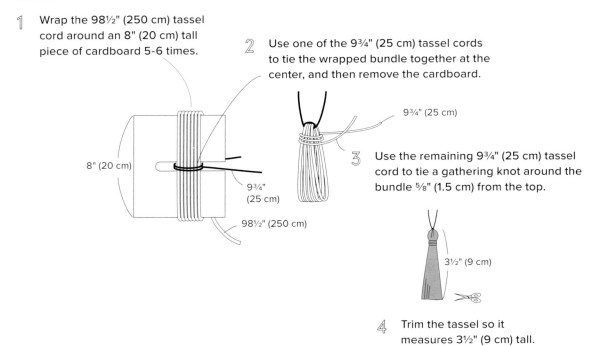

8" (20 cm)

9¾" (25 cm)

98½" (250 cm)

9¾" (25 cm)

3½" (9 cm)

4 Trim the tassel so it measures 3½" (9 cm) tall.

FINISH THE BAG

2 Tie the tassel to the zipper pull.

1 Hand stitch the zipper to the inside of the bag opening.

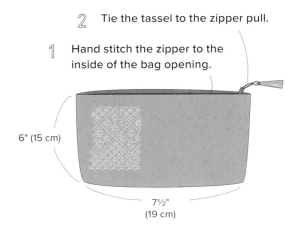

6" (15 cm)

7½" (19 cm)

12
Blue Diamond Tassel Clutch

Photo on page 33

MATERIALS

236¼ ft (72 m) of 2 mm aqua cotton cord

Working cords: 55" (140 cm) x 48 pieces
Filler cords: 19¾" (50 cm) x 2 pieces
Tassel cords: 98½" (250 cm) x 1 piece
                    9¾" (25 cm) x 2 pieces

One 7" (18 cm) zipper

SYMBOL KEY

Starting Method C
▷ *page 51*

Square Knot
▷ *page 56*

Reverse Horizontal Clove Hitch
▷ *page 62*

Horizontal Clove Hitch
▷ *page 60*

Diagonal Clove Hitch
▷ *page 62*

Square Knot
▷ *page 52*

Enclosed Clove Hitch
▷ *page 63*

Gathering Knot
▷ *page 53*

MAKE THE BAG BODY

1. Fold the 48 working cords in half at the center and attach to one of the filler cords using starting method C. Overlap the ends of the filler cord to form a loop and secure in place when attaching 4 of the working cords to the overlapped filler cord.

2. Knot 1 row of horizontal clove hitch and enclosed clove hitch, overlapping the ends of the filler cord to form a loop.

3. Knot 4 rows of single alternating square knots to form a treasure mesh pattern. Decrease the number of knots in each row. Make sure to join the ends together to create a tube-shaped bag.

4. Work diagonal clove hitch as noted in the diagram.

5. Make square knots using 4 strands as the filler cord.

6. Work reverse horizontal clove hitch as noted in the diagram.

7. Knot 11 rows of single alternating square knots to form a treasure mesh pattern. Decrease the number of knots starting at row 9.

8. Turn the bag inside out. Create the gussets by making square knots as indicated by the arrows where you see a ♡ symbol.

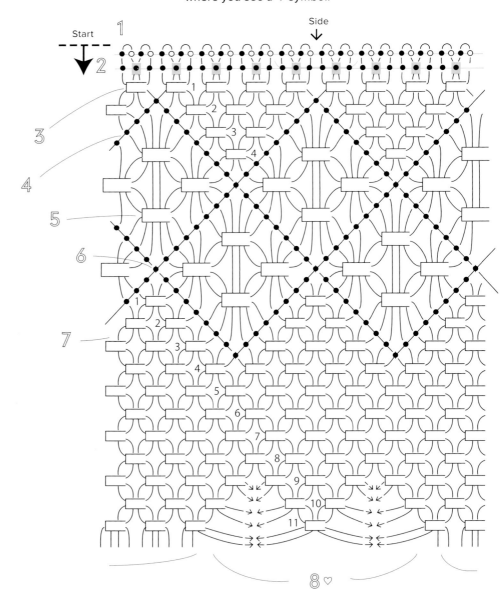

9. To form the bottom of the bag, make square knots with the opposite side of the bag where you see a ☆ symbol. Finish the cord ends as shown on page 71.

10. Make the tassel (refer to page 104 for instructions).

11. Hand stitch the zipper to the inside of the bag opening.

12. Tie the tassel to the zipper pull.

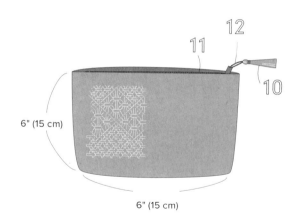

6" (15 cm)

6" (15 cm)

Side

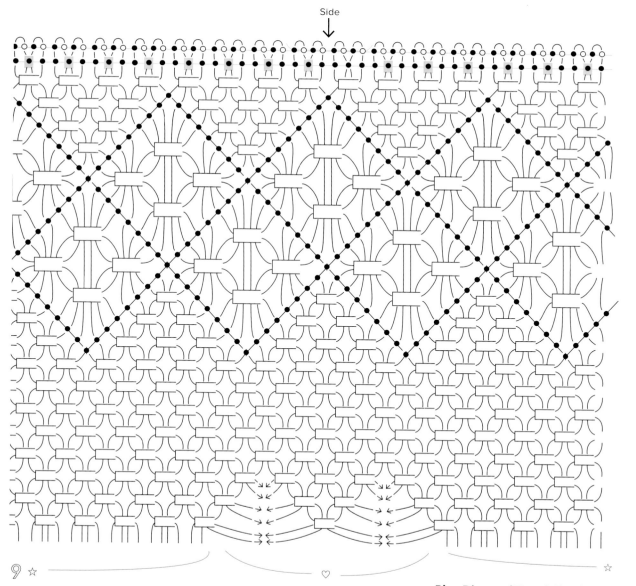

9 ☆   ♡   ☆

Blue Diamond Tassel Clutch

14 · 17
Zigzag Pattern Bag Strap & Belt

Photos on pages 36, 37 and 38

MATERIALS

FOR 14 (BAG STRAP)

131¼ ft (40 m) of 2 mm dark gray leather cord

> Working cords: 138" (350 cm) x 11 pieces
>
> Gathering knot cords: 23¾" (60 cm)
> x 2 pieces

½ yd (0.5 m) of canvas fabric

Two sets of ¾" (2 cm) diameter grommets

FOR 17 (BELT)

95¼ ft (29 m) of 2 mm light gray leather cord

> Working cords: 98½" (250 cm) x 11 pieces
>
> Gathering knot cords: 23¾" (60 cm)
> x 2 pieces

MAKE THE BAG STRAP/BELT

1. Align the 11 working cords. Starting from the center, knot 13¾" (35 cm) of diagonal clove hitch for the bag strap or 8" (20 cm) for the belt. Return to the center and follow the same process to knot the other side.

2. Use the remaining cords to make ⅝" (1.5 cm) gathering knots at each end.

3. Trim the excess cord to 23¾" (60 cm).

SYMBOL KEY

  Diagonal Clove Hitch
▷ *page 62*

 Gathering Knot
▷ *page 53*

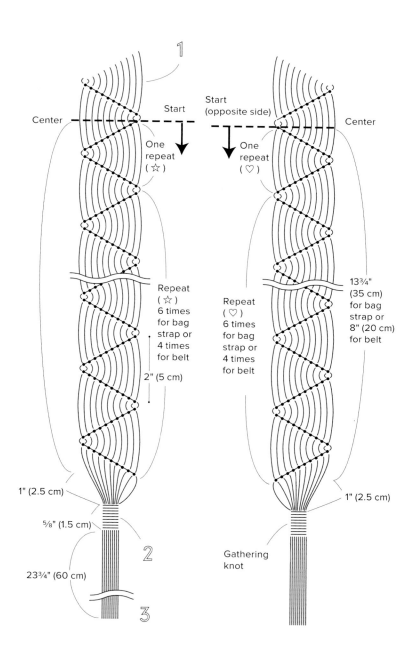

1

Center | Start

Start (opposite side) | Center

One repeat (☆)

One repeat (♡)

Repeat (☆) 6 times for bag strap or 4 times for belt

2" (5 cm)

Repeat (♡) 6 times for bag strap or 4 times for belt

13¾" (35 cm) for bag strap or 8" (20 cm) for belt

1" (2.5 cm)

⅝" (1.5 cm)

2

23¾" (60 cm)

3

1" (2.5 cm)

Gathering knot

Zigzag Pattern Bag Strap & Belt

MAKE THE BAG (FOR 14 ONLY)

1 Cut a 15¾" x 35½" (40 x 90 cm) rectangle of fabric and fold in half.

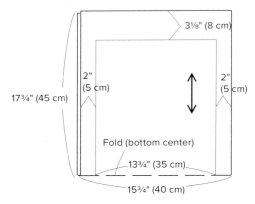

3⅛" (8 cm)

2" (5 cm)

2" (5 cm)

17¾" (45 cm)

Fold (bottom center)

13¾" (35 cm)

15¾" (40 cm)

2 Fold the long edges over ⅜" (1 cm) and press with the iron. Note that one edge should be folded over to the wrong side and the opposite edge should be folded over to the right side.

⅜" (1 cm)

⅜" (1 cm)

(WS)

1¼" (3 cm)

(WS)

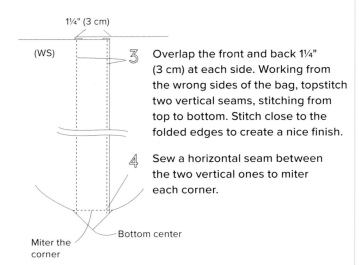

3 Overlap the front and back 1¼" (3 cm) at each side. Working from the wrong sides of the bag, topstitch two vertical seams, stitching from top to bottom. Stitch close to the folded edges to create a nice finish.

4 Sew a horizontal seam between the two vertical ones to miter each corner.

Miter the corner

Bottom center

5 Turn the bag right side out. Fold the opening edge over ⅜" (1 cm) and press. Next, fold it over another 2¾" (7 cm) and press. Topstitch to finish the opening.

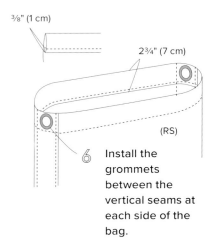

⅜" (1 cm)

2¾" (7 cm)

(RS)

6 Install the grommets between the vertical seams at each side of the bag.

7 Insert the fringe through the grommets and tie to secure the bag strap in place.

13¾" (35 cm)

12¼" (31 cm)

Six Strand Braid Bag Strap & Belt

Photos on pages 37, 38 and 39

MATERIALS

Color A: 12¼ ft (3.7 m) of 2 mm light gray leather cord

Color B: 24½ ft (7.4 m) of 2 mm dark brown leather cord

  Color A: 145¾" (370 cm) x 1 piece
  Color B: 145¾" (370 cm) x 2 pieces

One 1½" x 1¼" (4 x 3 cm) wooden ring

FOR 15 (BAG) ONLY

Reusable bag

Two 3⅛" (8 cm) pieces of ⅝" (1.5 cm) wide twill tape

One set of snaps

SYMBOL KEY

 Starting Method A
▷ *page 50*

 Overhand Knot
▷ *page 52*

 Six Strand Braid
▷ *page 55*

MAKE THE BAG STRAP/BELT

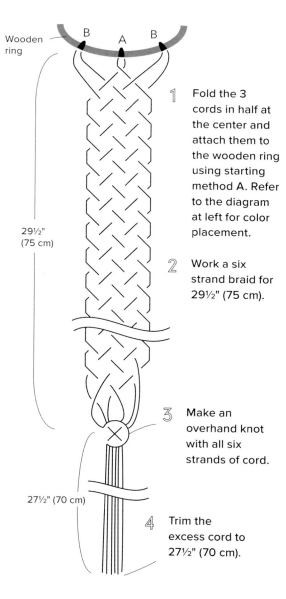

Wooden ring

29½" (75 cm)

27½" (70 cm)

1 Fold the 3 cords in half at the center and attach them to the wooden ring using starting method A. Refer to the diagram at left for color placement.

2 Work a six strand braid for 29½" (75 cm).

3 Make an overhand knot with all six strands of cord.

4 Trim the excess cord to 27½" (70 cm).

MAKE THE BAG
(FOR 15 ONLY)

1   Cut the existing handle off your reusable bag.

3   Insert the fringe through the twill tape loop and tie to secure the bag strap in place.

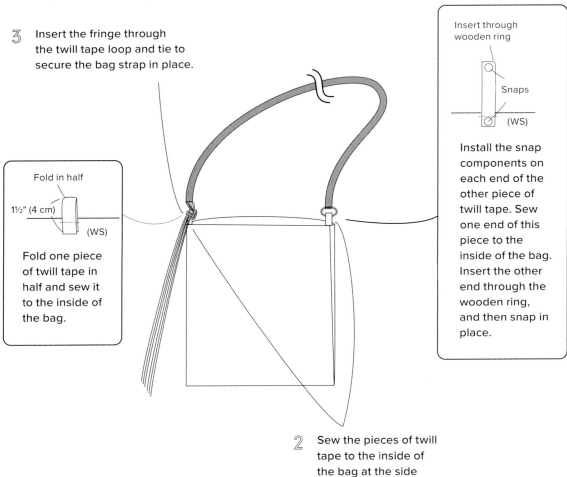

Insert through wooden ring

Snaps

(WS)

Install the snap components on each end of the other piece of twill tape. Sew one end of this piece to the inside of the bag. Insert the other end through the wooden ring, and then snap in place.

Fold in half

1½" (4 cm)

(WS)

Fold one piece of twill tape in half and sew it to the inside of the bag.

2   Sew the pieces of twill tape to the inside of the bag at the side seams.

18

Fringe Shoulder Bag

Photo on page 40

MATERIALS

403¾ ft (123 m) of 2 mm off-white cotton cord

Working cords: 78¾" (200 cm) x 48 pieces
Filler cords: 19¾" (50 cm) x 2 pieces
Handle cords: 141¾" (360 cm) x 4 pieces
                 106½" (270 cm) x 4 pieces

Lining fabric: ⅛ yd (0.3 m)

Fusible interfacing: 7¼" x 2½" (18 x 6 cm)

One ¾" (2 cm) diameter magnetic button

SYMBOL KEY

 Starting Method C
▷ *page 51*

 Square Knot
▷ *page 56*

 Diagonal Clove Hitch
▷ *page 62*

 Enclosed Clove Hitch
▷ *page 63*

 Horizontal Clove Hitch
▷ *page 60*

 Slip Knot
▷ *page 53*

MAKE THE HANDLE

1 Align the handle cords at the center, as shown in the diagram below.

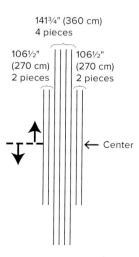

141¾" (360 cm)
4 pieces

106½"
(270 cm)
2 pieces

106½"
(270 cm)
2 pieces

← Center

2 Starting from the center and working toward each end separately, knot single alternating square knots to form a treasure mesh pattern for 22" (56 cm).

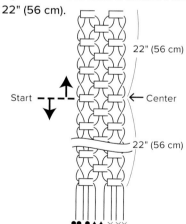

22" (56 cm)

Start

← Center

22" (56 cm)

3 When the bag body is complete, insert the cord ends through the bag body, aligning the symbols noted in the diagrams (see pages 114-115). Tie square knots on the inside of the bag to secure the handle in place.

MAKE THE BAG BODY

1. Fold the 48 working cords in half at the center and attach to one of the filler cords using starting method C. Overlap the ends of the filler cord to form a loop and secure in place when attaching 4 of the working cords to the overlapped filler cord.

2. Knot 7 rows of single alternating square knots to form a treasure mesh pattern. Make sure to join the ends together to create a tube-shaped bag.

3. Knot 1 row of horizontal clove hitch and enclosed clove hitch, overlapping the ends of the filler cord to form a loop.

4. Knot 4 rows of single alternating square knots to form a treasure mesh pattern. Next, work diagonal clove hitch as noted in the diagram.

5. Make square knots using 6 strands as the filler cord.

6. Knot 11 rows of single alternating square knots to form a treasure mesh pattern.

7. To form the bottom of the bag, bundle the cords together in groups of 8 (4 cords from each side of the bag). Secure each bundle with a slip knot using one of the cords. Apply a dab of glue to each knot. Trim the fringe to 7" (18 cm).

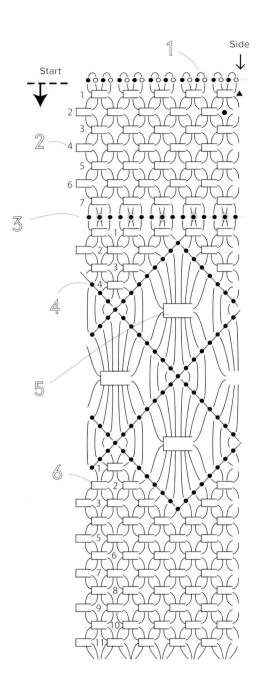

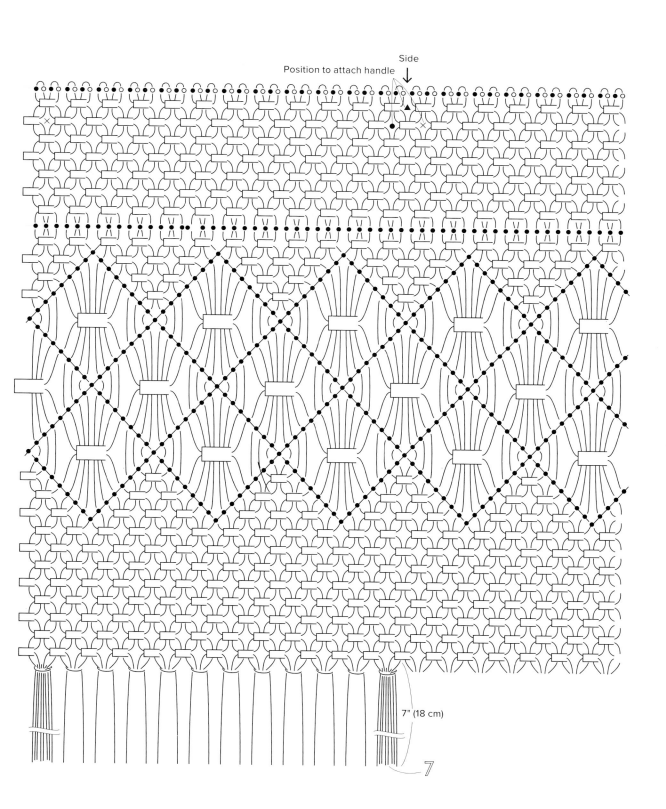

Side

Position to attach handle

7" (18 cm)

7

MAKE THE LINING

1. Cut an 8" x 18" (20 x 46 cm) rectangle of fabric.

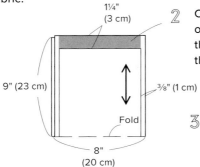

1¼"
(3 cm)

9" (23 cm)

⅜" (1 cm)

Fold

8"
(20 cm)

2. Cut two 1¼" x 7¼" (3 x 18 cm) pieces of fusible interfacing and adhere to the wrong side of the fabric along the top and bottom edges.

3. Fold in half with wrong sides together. Sew along the sides using ⅛" (3 mm) seam allowance.

4. Turn the bag inside out and sew along each side again, using ¼" (5 mm) seam allowance this time to create a French seam.

5. Fold the top 1¼" (3 cm) of the bag opening to the wrong side and press.

(RS)

8" (20 cm)

(WS)

¼" (5 mm)

4

(WS)

3

7"
(18 cm)

6. Insert the lining into the bag body and hand stitch together around the opening.

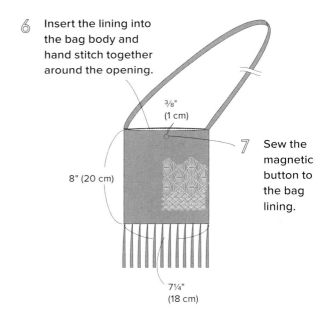

⅜"
(1 cm)

8" (20 cm)

7. Sew the magnetic button to the bag lining.

7¼"
(18 cm)

19 · 20
Nylon & Jute Flat Bags

Photos on page 42

MATERIALS

650 ft (198 m) of 2.5 mm navy blue nylon cord (for 19)
or 650 ft (198 m) of 2.5 mm jute/bamboo cord (for 20)

- Working cords: 51¼" (130 cm) x 112 pieces
- Filler cords: 39½" (100 cm) x 2 pieces
- Bag opening cords: 16½ ft (5 m) x 10 pieces

SYMBOL KEY

Square Knot
▷ *page 56*

Spiral Knot
▷ *page 58*

Horizontal Clove Hitch
▷ *page 60*

Square Knot
▷ *page 52*

FINISHED DIAGRAM

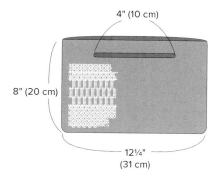

4" (10 cm)

8" (20 cm)

12¼"
(31 cm)

MAKE THE BAG BODY

1. Fold two pieces of bag opening cord in half at the center (this is one set). Align 5 sets as shown in the diagram below and knot 112 rows of single alternating square knots to form a treasure mesh pattern. Make holes for the handles following the placement noted in the diagram. Insert the cord ends through the square knots of the first row to form a loop (refer to the diagram at right).

2. Attach the working cords to the piece from step 1 (refer to the diagram below). Knot 2 rows of single alternating square knots to form a treasure mesh pattern. Make sure to join the ends together to create a tube-shaped bag.

How to Make a Loop in Step 1

Insert the cord ends through the starting loops, and make square knots, connecting the cords indicated by the arrows.

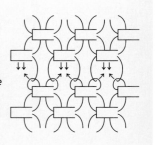

How to Attach the Cords in Step 2

Insert the working cords through the loops and fold in half at the center.

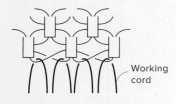

Working cord

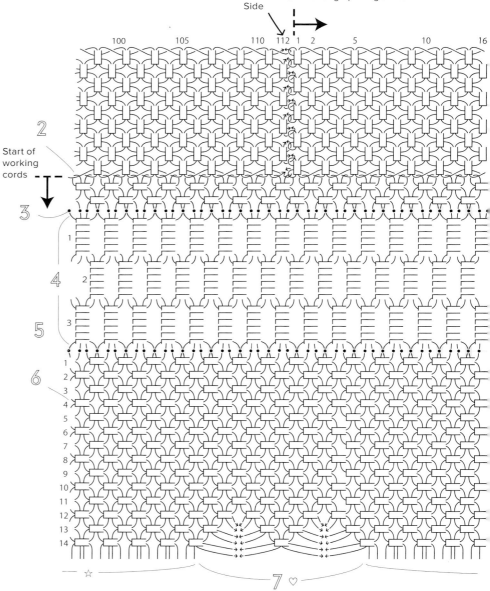

Side

Start of bag opening cords

Start of working cords

Macramé Bags

3. Knot 1 row of horizontal clove hitch, overlapping the ends of the filler cord to form a loop.

4. Knot 3 rows of 6 left facing alternating spiral knots to form a treasure mesh pattern.

5. Repeat step 3.

6. Knot 14 rows of single alternating square knots to form a treasure mesh pattern. Decrease the number of knots starting at row 12.

7. Turn the bag inside out. Create the gussets by making square knots where you see a ♡ symbol.

8. To form the bottom of the bag, make square knots with the opposite side of the bag where you see a ☆ symbol. Finish the cord ends as shown on page 71.

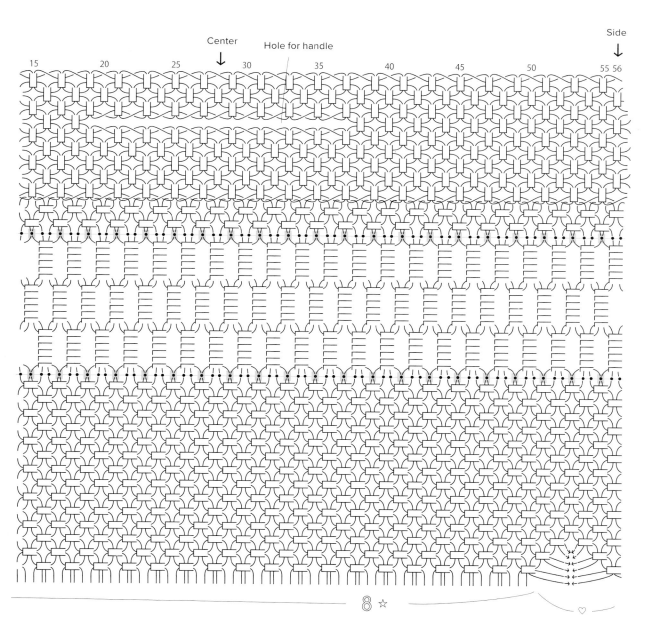

21
Vintage-Inspired Handbag

Photo on page 45

MATERIALS

613½ ft (187 m) of 2 mm cotton cord
> Working cords: 71" (180 cm) x 100 pieces
> Filler cords: 15¾" (40 cm) x 5 pieces
> Tab cords: 19¾" (50 cm) x 6 pieces
> Button cords: 11¾" (30 cm) x 4 pieces

39½" (100 cm) of 3 mm diameter braided leather cord

> *For this project, you'll start by making the bag body as noted on pages 122-123. Next you'll make the tab, button, and strap as noted on page 121, and attach them to the bag body.*

SYMBOL KEY

Starting Method B
▷ *page 50*

Horizontal Clove Hitch
▷ *page 60*

Square Knot
▷ *page 56*

Enclosed Clove Hitch
▷ *page 63*

Slip Knot
▷ *page 53*

Berry Knot
▷ *page 57*

Diagonal Clove Hitch
▷ *page 62*

Square Knot
▷ *page 52*

Crown Knot
▷ *page 59*

MAKE THE TAB

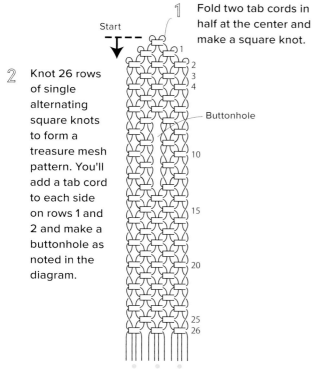

Start

1 Fold two tab cords in half at the center and make a square knot.

2 Knot 26 rows of single alternating square knots to form a treasure mesh pattern. You'll add a tab cord to each side on rows 1 and 2 and make a buttonhole as noted in the diagram.

Buttonhole

3 Insert the cord ends through the bag body at the positions marked with pink circle symbols (refer to diagram on pages 122–123). Make square knots on the wrong side of the bag to secure in place.

ADD THE STRAP

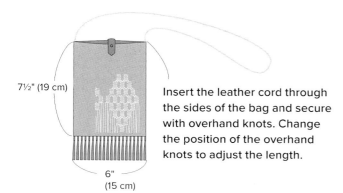

7½" (19 cm)

6"
(15 cm)

Insert the leather cord through the sides of the bag and secure with overhand knots. Change the position of the overhand knots to adjust the length.

MAKE THE BUTTON

Arrange the 4 strands of button cord in a cross shape, with 2 strands in each direction. Make a crown knot as shown on page 59. Insert the cord ends through the bag body at the position marked with pink triangle symbols (refer to diagram on pages 122-123). Make square knots on the wrong side of the bag to secure in place.

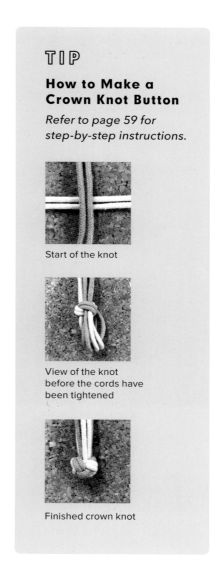

TIP

How to Make a Crown Knot Button

Refer to page 59 for step-by-step instructions.

Start of the knot

View of the knot before the cords have been tightened

Finished crown knot

MAKE THE BAG BODY

1. Fold the 100 working cords in half at the center and attach to one of the filler cords using starting method B. Overlap the ends of the filler cord to form a loop and secure in place when attaching 4 of the working cords to the overlapped filler cord.

2. Knot 1 row of horizontal clove hitch and enclosed horizontal clove hitch, overlapping the ends of the filler cord to form a loop.

3. Knot 3 rows of triple alternating square knots to form a treasure mesh pattern. Make sure to join the ends together to create a tube-shaped bag.

4. Make 10 left facing spiral knots using adjacent sets of working cords.

5. Make 1 square knot using adjacent sets of working cords.

6. Repeat step 2, making sure to shift the placement of the overlapped filler cord slightly.

7. Make square knots as noted in the diagram.

8. Knot 3 rows of diagonal clove hitch as noted in the diagram.

9. Make a berry knot with 6 square knots as noted in the diagram.

    [Repeat steps 8, 7, 5, and 6 as noted in the diagram]

10. Knot 9 rows of triple alternating square knots to form a treasure mesh pattern.

    [Repeat step 6 as noted in the diagram]

11. Knot 2 rows of triple alternating square knots to form a treasure mesh pattern.

12. Bundle the corresponding square knot cords together on the front and back of the bag, as indicated by the ★.

13. Make 2.5 square knots. Bundle 8 cords together and make a slip knot using one of the cords. Apply a dab of glue to each knot. Trim the excess cord, leaving 1½" (4 cm) of fringe.

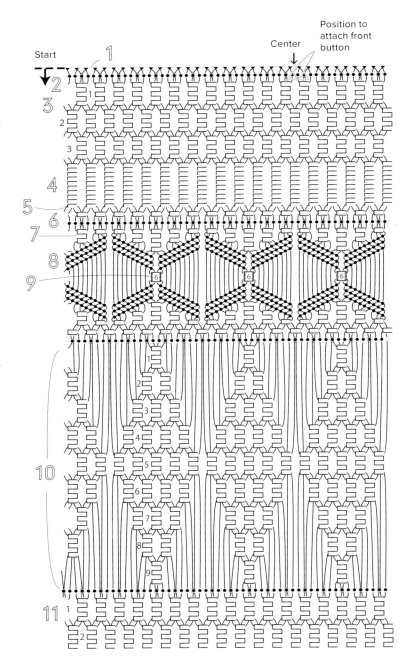

Side Position to attach tab Center Side

12 ★ 13

1½"
(4 cm)

Macramé Pattern Inspiration Gallery

nce you've mastered the basic knots, try combining different techniques to create macramé patterns with interesting shapes and textures. Use the following inspiration gallery as a reference when designing your own macramé projects.

Treasure Mesh Patterns without Gaps

Square Knots

This is the most basic form of treasure mesh pattern and is made with alternating square knots without leaving gaps between each row.

One Square Knot + Two Square Knots

Despite the fact that there are still no gaps between the rows, this variation has a sheer look due to the increased number of square knots.

Square Knot + Alternating Half Hitch Knot

Create a soft, nubby texture by incorporating alternating half hitch knots into the treasure mesh pattern.

Treasure Mesh Patterns with Gaps

Leave Areas without Knots

Combine areas with and without knotwork to create an airy, open feeling.

Leaves Small Spaces Between Knots

Leave just a small gap between the knots for a sheer, light feeling.

Leave Larger Spaces Between Knots

Create this interesting, spacious effect utilizing alternating triple square knots.

Spiral Knots

Square Knot + Spiral Knot

Use spiral knots in between a treasure mesh pattern made with square knots to create a sheer three-dimensional look.

Treasure Mesh Pattern Using Spiral Knots

Make alternating spiral knots to create a three-dimensional net-like texture.

Two Spiral Knots + Three Square Knots

Use three square knots to increase the openness. This technique can even be used to create a belt loop.

Diagonal Clove Hitch

Round Flower Pattern

This is a more advanced technique which involves knotting alternating diagonal clove hitch in a spiral. The square knots in between the spirals are reminiscent of petals.

Diamond Pattern

Work diagonal clove hitch in a rhombus shape to create a geometric pattern.

Basketweave Pattern

Work alternating diagonal clove hitch to create a beautiful textured pattern inspired by a woven basket.

Zigzag Pattern

This dynamic zigzag pattern is created with diagonal clove hitch. The square knots between zigzags make the linear design stand out.

Leaf Pattern

Work diagonal clove hitch in a curved pattern to create shapes evocative of gently falling leaves. The gradually curved cords between the leaf designs form a beautiful background.

Berry Knot

Dot Pattern

Three-dimensional berry knots create a playful, popcorn-like pattern. Use this design as an accent as it creates a thick fabric.

Afterword

Macramé is created by making one knot at a time.

I hope this book inspires you to connect more than just cords, but also to connect with the hearts and minds of others.

I find the process of macramé quite meditative and try to keep these loving thoughts in mind as I work.

About 40 years ago, the late Ms. Keiko Oka learned the art of macramé while traveling in the US and brought her newfound passion back to Japan.

In order to share her love of macramé with others, she established the Japan Macramé Association and began drafting macramé diagrams using symbols.

I would like to express my gratitude to Ms. Keiko Oka and those who read this book, as well as those who have been involved in making this book.

Chizu Takuma

Resources

Etsy

www.etsy.com
Online marketplace offering macramé cord in a variety of colors and weights, as well as leather handles, grommets, rivets, and other bag findings

Fancy Tiger Crafts Cooperative

www.fancytigercrafts.com
Independent craft shop offering macramé and bag making supplies

Hobby Lobby

www.hobbylobby.com
National craft supply chain that sells a variety of macramé cords and bag findings

JoAnn

www.joann.com
National craft supply chain that sells a variety of macramé cords and bag findings

Michaels

www.michaels.com
National craft supply chain that sells a variety of macramé cords and bag findings

Modern Macramé

www.modernmacrame.com
Online macramé community and shop

Niroma Studio

www.niromastudio.com
Offers high quality macramé supplies

Paracord Planet

www.paracordplanet.com
Online site offering a variety of macramé cord, as well as tools and supplies, including macramé boards, T-pins, wooden rings, bag handles, D-rings, and more

Rock Mountain Co.

www.rockmountain.co
Offers high quality macramé supplies